P9-DGI-522

NATURE CRAFTS WITH A *Microwave*

Art Director: Dana Irwin
Photography: Evan Bracken, Light Reflections
Production: Elaine Thompson
Proofreading: Julie Brown

Library of Congress Cataloging-in-Publication Data

Cusick, Dawn
Nature crafts with a microwave : over 80 projects / by Dawn Cusick.
p. cm.
"A Sterling/Lark book."
Includes index.
ISBN 0-8069-0666-9
1. Nature craft. 2. Microwave ovens. 3. Plants—Drying.
4. Potpourris (Scented floral mixtures) I. Title.
TT157.C79 1994
745.5—dc 20 94–776
CIP

10 9 8 7 6 5 4

A Sterling/Lark Book

First paperback edition published in 1995 by
Sterling Publishing Company, Inc.
387 Park Avenue South, New York, N.Y. 10016

Produced by Altamont Press, Inc.
50 College Street, Asheville, NC 28801

Distributed in Canada by Sterling Publishing
℅ Canadian Manda Group, One Atlantic Avenue, Suite 105
Toronto, Ontario, Canada M6K 3E7
Distributed in Great Britain and Europe by Cassell PLC
Villiers House, 41/47 Strand, London WC2N 5JE, England
Distributed in Australia by Capricorn Link (Australia) Pty Ltd.
P.O. Box 6651, Baulkham Hills, Business Centre,
NSW 2153, Australia

Every effort has been made to ensure that all the information in this book is accurate. However, due to differing conditions, tools, and individual skills, the publisher cannot be responsible for any injuries, losses, and other damages which may result from the use of the information in this book.

Sterling ISBN 0-8069-0666-9 Trade
0-8069-0667-7 Paper

NATURE CRAFTS WITH A *Microwave*

DAWN CUSICK

A Sterling/Lark Book
Sterling Publishing Co., Inc. New York

Contents

Contributing Designers

NORA BLOSE is a frequent contributor to craft books and coauthor of *The Herb Drying Handbook* (Sterling Publishing, 1992). She markets her herbal crafts under the name "Nora's Follies," and frequently shares her love of herbs with garden clubs and school groups. (Pages 34, 41, 44, 54, 55, 57, and 65 - 67.)

JULIANNE BRONDER lives in Downer's Grove, Illinois, where she creates a variety of innovative nature projects for craft books. (Pages 32, 42, 79, and 106.)

ALICE ENSLEY enjoys dabbling in a wide variety of crafts, from sewing to nature crafts, as well as experimenting with new materials. She lives in Candler, North Carolina, with her husband and five children. (Pages 24 - 27, 35, and 100.)

JUDITH FOX creates her cornshuck dolls and flowers for a wide range of international clients. She lives in Morristown, Tennessee, where she grows herbs and flowers for her business, Willow Hill Farm, and teaches craft workshops. (Pages 120 - 123.)

DIANE GRINNELL's background in fashion and graphic design led her to the Penland School of Crafts in Western North Carolina, where she currently resides. She designs and produces surface designed textiles, and has a production line of household linens for the kitchen, dining room, and bedroom. (Pages 90 - 93.)

JUDY MALLOW is a third-generation pine needle crafter from Carthage, North Carolina. In addition to making a wide range of pine needle baskets, she also enjoys playing with other natural materials and techniques. (Pages 72, 73, 124, and 125.)

DOLLY LUTZ MORRIS lives in rural Pennsylvania with her husband and five children. She markets her handmade dolls, painted furniture, and dried flower crafts in her shop, 219 Market Square, in Meadville, Pennsylvania. (Pages 28, 33, 36, 51, and 119.)

ALYCE NADEAU grows more than 200 varieties of herbs for her herbal craft business, Goldenrod Mountain Herbs, in Deep Gap, North Carolina. She is presently working on her first book, a guide to starting a small herb business, for Sterling Publishing, available in 1995. (Pages 23, 30, 31, 46, 48, 50, 53, 56, 58 - 61, 63, 64, 70, 74 -78, 87 - 89, 96, and 107.)

MARY WOJECK is a gourd crafter from Traveller's Rest, South Carolina. She especially enjoys creating fanciful animals from gourds, and her work has been on display in the Museum of Natural Science. (Pages 82, 86, 118, and 119.)

TOMMY WOLFF lives in the mountains of Western North Carolina, where he enjoys relaxing with craft projects after long days as a marketing executive in the banking industry. (Pages 104, 105, 108 - 111, 114, 116, and 117.)

*Also thanks to...*CYNTHIA GILLOOLY (pages 45, 68, 81, 95, 102), DEBORAH HENDERSON, Sweets and Feasts (pages 108, 109), WANA HENRY (page 97 - 99), LINDA LOVE (page 69), JANIE MARKLEY (page 112), CHRIS MARKS (page 80), JAMIE MCCABE (page 115), NANCY MCCAULEY (pages 37 and 40), KIT MECKLY (page 85), ETHEL ROBERSON (page 30), SYLVIA TIPPETT (page 29), and DIANE WEAVER (page 38).

Introduction

It's amazing to think that ten years ago most people had never heard of a microwave oven. Today, they're a mainstay in most kitchens. I chuckle to think that 40 or 50 years from now I may be telling my grandchildren about the days when we "cooked meals the hard way, on an electric stove." (I hope they'll be kinder to me than my brother and I were to my grandfather as he told childhood tales of using outhouses and walking to school every day 12 miles in the snow.)

The basic instructions and craft projects should provide you with enough information and motivation to successfully complete a variety of decorative and useful items. But don't stop there. The beauty of microwave drying is that there's a world of undiscovered possibilities out there, and it only takes a few minutes — in between defrosting the roast and cooking the corn — for experimenting. When looking through possible projects to make, don't worry if you're missing some of the materials. Just use the instructions as a guideline and have fun searching for substitute materials with great colors and shapes. You'll be thrilled with the results.

When working with a new material, try not to be intimidated by the time ranges suggested in the basic instructions. Differences can be influenced by a number of variables: the wattage of your microwave (unlike a toothbrush, they're not all basically the same), the amount of moisture in the item you're working with (the rainstorm that drenched your roses last night may well add two or three minutes to the cooking time), and the specific dimensions of the materials (size, thickness, etc.). Learning to microwave natural materials follows precisely the same pattern as learning to microwave foods — at first you'll feel like everything's guesswork, then all of a sudden it will just make sense.

A special thanks is extended here to all of the adventuresome, talented designers who shared their crafts and techniques.

Microwaving Natural Materials

Microwave Mechanics

You needn't become a scientist specializing in radioactive waves to successfully prepare natural materials in the microwave. It helps, though, to have a basic idea of how the process works. If you're microwaving seven or eight orange slices, it's important to know, for instance, that the slices closest to the walls will receive the most energy, and may develop burn spots long before the slices in the middle are dry unless you rotate positions halfway through the cooking time. Other technical information may prove equally helpful, so try to resist the temptation to skip this section.

Microwaves

Microwaves are actually short radio waves, which, like light waves, may be reflected and concentrated. Unlike light waves, though, they are able to pass through the ionosphere, a fact which subjected them to intensive research from scientists looking for waves able to conduct satellites and plane navigation during the second world war.

In a microwave oven, microwaves are generated in special types of electron tubes called magnetron tubes. The microwaves generated by these tubes are then scattered through the oven by a small fan. The microwaves bounce off the oven's walls, pass through any paper, plastic, or glass products, and enter the food. As they enter the food, the microwaves cause the liquid molecules to vibrate, thus producing heat. Items placed closest to the oven's walls will heat faster, since they're closest to the area where the microwaves first hit. Since microwaves create heat fastest in items with the most liquid, you shouldn't try to dry different materials — such as roses and strawflowers — in the same batch.

Standing Time

Because the molecules in a particular material will still be moving at increased speeds when you remove the material from the microwave, the item will technically continue to "cook" for a few minutes. Thus, to prevent over drying, you'll need to allow for a few minutes of standing time after every cooking session. Place a lid on your container and leave it vented a little during this period. (If you're using a brown paper bag, unroll one end a little.)

Basic Materials

Microwave Oven

You don't need a fancy, ultra-expensive oven to prepare natural materials for crafts. Ideally, though, it helps to have at least two wattage settings, which may be labeled on your microwave oven as defrost/cook, high/low, or numerically 1 - 10.

Microwave Paper Towels

Paper towels are used to absorb moisture from the items being dried. When purchasing paper towels for microwave craft use, chose a towel without color prints that does not contain recycled fibers. (The recycled fibers ignite sooner, and could be a fire hazard.) If you prefer, there are several brands of paper towels labeled specifically for use in the microwave.

Brown Paper Bag

You don't need to search for anything special here; an ordinary brown lunch bag works just fine. As with paper towels, though, be sure not to use paper bags made from recycled fibers. To dry flowers or herbs in a brown bag, open the bag and place sev-

eral blooms inside. Gently fold up the ends, and then place the bag on top of a microwave-safe bowl. (The bowl allows any accumulating moisture to drain downward, instead of dampening the flowers.) Brown bags are also used when working with materials that you'd prefer not touch your cooking surfaces, such as mosses and cones.

Cake Rack

An ordinary metal cake rack is useful to have on hand. When working with easy-to-burn materials

like citrus and apple slices, you may choose to do the bulk of the drying in the microwave and allow them to finish drying on the cake rack.

Silica Gel

Silica gel is a moisture-absorbing desiccant, and can usually be found in craft stores. To dry flowers or herbs in the microwave with silica gel, first line the bottom of a microwave-safe container with a 1-inch-thick layer of the silica crystals. Arrange the flowers on top of the silica gel, allowing about an inch of space around the sides and between each flower. Cover with another 1-inch-thick layer of silica gel, then microwave on 50% power for 3 minutes. Check the materials' progress, and add more time in short increments if needed. After you've experimented with materials and times, you'll be able to dry several layers of flowers at the same time. Since silica gel often absorbs pesticides from plants as they dry, you may feel safer reserving this container exclusively for drying flowers in the microwave.

Some success tips: Since flowers and leaves often have different drying times, you'll probably want to remove the leaves and microwave them separately; take care not to breathe in the powders that may rise up as you pour silica gel into a container (they can irritate the nasal passage); never use silica gel on anything damp or wet (it just cooks into the material); an inexpensive child's paintbrush makes a good tool for brushing crystals off from delicate dried flowers; check the manufacturer's instructions for specific directions for recycling moisture-saturated crystals.

What to Expect

Shrinkage

As their moisture evaporates through drying in the microwave, materials will shrink in size. The precise amount of shrinkage is impossible to predict. Some materials, such as strawflowers, for instance, shrink very little; while others, such as daffodils, shrink substantially. Shrinkage is not a problem in itself, but if you're making a large project, such as a wreath, you'll need to dry extra materials.

Color Changes

Like shrinkage, color changes vary from material to material. Foliage tends to darken a little, as do many flowers. A few materials will surprise you and keep exactly the same color, while others may even brighten a little.

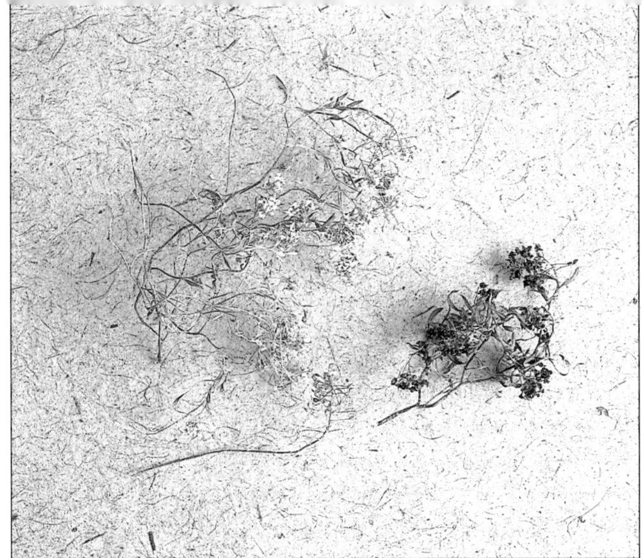

Shape Changes

Most materials change shape to some degree. Petals and leaves usually curl upward, although in some cases, such as with wet pinecones, the cones' petals will unfold downward as they dry.

Burning

Burn marks usually show up first in the center of the material, such as a citrus slice, and work outward. If the marks are very small, you can usually scrape them off with the blade of a craft knife. If your materials get burn marks, be sure to note the times and wattages used so you can make appropriate time reductions next time.

Fragrance Changes

Because fragrance comes from a plant's natural oils, it makes sense that much of the fragrance will dissipate as moisture evaporates during microwave cooking. Especially pungent plants, such as rosemary, will still have fragrance; while many of the milder fragrances, such as tarragon, will disappear.

Safety

Because microwaving creates such high internal temperatures, be sure to handle recently microwaved materials with tongs or protected hands. Before you begin working, check your home's fuse box and take note of which circuit your microwave is on. If some of your materials catch on fire, avoid the temptation to open the oven's door, which would only fuel the fire with a nice burst of fresh oxygen. Instead, turn off the power at the fuse box or unplug the cord. Also, since many items accumulate steam as they cook, take care to protect your face when opening bags of popcorn or other materials.

Microwave drying is certainly miraculous, but it's definitely not an exact science. The amount of moisture a particular material contains, along with the varying wattages of microwaves, makes predicting exact drying times impossible. Perhaps it can best be compared to baking a lemon meringue pie. The difference in time between achieving a golden brown meringue and burned peaks is difficult to predict and minimal. After a few test batches, though, you'll feel like an expert, and develop a sense of how much time will achieve good results. If you're not in the mood to waste fruit and electricity experimenting, though, you can always remove your natural materials just before they're completely dry and allow them to finish drying for a day or two on a cake rack.

Fruits and Vegetables

Select fruits and vegetables for drying as though you were buying food for an exquisite dinner party. Fruits and vegetables should be ripe (to ensure good color), but not too ripe, with no visible surface bruises or discolorations.

Citrus Fruits

Oranges, lemons, grapefruit, and limes all dry well in the microwave and even retain a little of their noteworthy fragrances. Lemon slices are not as attractive as the other fruits, but they emit a wonderful, fresh fragrance as they dry and leave you with a shining clean microwave.

To begin, slice the fruit in 1/8- to 1/4-inch (3 to 6 mm) widths and arrange them on three layers of microwavable paper towels. Cover with two more towels and microwave at 50% power. Turn the fruit over, placing them in a dry area of the towels, and microwave again. Replace the bottom paper towels with dry ones if they become too wet. Remove the fruit before burn marks start to appear. Time Ranges: Oranges, 4 slices, 8 minutes at 50% power, turning halfway through. Lemons and limes, 4 slices, 6 minutes at 50% power, turning halfway through. Grapefruit, 3 slices, 10 minutes at 50% power, turning halfway through.

Apples

Apple slices dry well and have multiple craft uses. You can remove the core or leave the seeds in place, as you like. After slicing the fruit in 1/8- to 1/4-inch slices, sprinkle both sides with lemon juice to prevent discoloration and allow the juice to dry for a few minutes. Arrange the slices on paper towels as directed for citrus fruits and microwave on 50% power for 4 minutes on each side, replacing the bottom paper towels with dry ones if they become too damp. As the apple slices dry, watch for color changes. The dry areas will not look distinctive, but the undry areas (usually the area around the cored holes) will look moist like applesauce.

Kiwi

Native to the forests in China's Yangtse Valley, this tender green fruit retains its color fairly well if sprinkled with a little lemon juice before microwaving. Slice the fruit in 1/8-inch thicknesses and arrange it on three layers of paper towels. Cover with two more layers of paper towels and microwave for 6 minutes on 50% power, turning halfway through and replacing the bottom paper towels with dry ones if they become too damp. Add additional time if needed and watch closely for burn spots.

Gourds

Although gourd crafting is an ancient art, dating back to early Indian cultures across several continents, gourds are gaining a newfound, and much deserved, public appreciation. Successful microwave gourd drying is good news, because air-drying takes a long time. Also, when crafters air-dry their gourds, they must purchase them directly from farmers to ensure they haven't been sprayed with wax or another substance which can prevent drying and cause the gourds to rot. With the microwave, though, grocery store gourds can be dried with ease. Gourds will darken slightly in color as they dry in the microwave.

Look for gourds in all sorts of shapes, spoon-shaped gourds, egg-shaped gourds, pear-shaped gourds, etc. Obviously, you're limited by the size that will fit in your microwave. First, drill 1/2-inch holes in both ends of the gourds. Place them in the microwave on paper towels and microwave for 15 minutes on one-third power or defrost cycle. Cooking too fast will make them shrivel, so don't be tempted to use full power. Make a mental note of how heavy the gourd feels before you place it in the oven; it will feel much lighter as the water evaporates out of the gourd.

Corn

Both the husks and the kernels can be prepared for craft projects in the microwave. To microwave the kernels for popcorn, it's best to avoid the safety hazards of popping the kernels in a brown lunch bag. Follow the manufacturer's instructions for time and power guidelines.

To prepare cornhusks for craft use, place them in a large microwavable container, cover them with water, and add 2 tablespoons of bleach. Soak for two hours, then microwave with a cover for 12 minutes on 50% power.

Chili Peppers

The deep red color of these peppers and their interesting shape make them an attractive addition to many craft projects, especially those designed to decorate the kitchen. To dry the peppers, make several small holes with a needle at the top and bottom of the pepper. Microwave them on 50% power between single layers of paper towels for 3 minutes, turning halfway through. Allow the peppers to finish drying outside of the microwave to prevent excessive shriveling.

Zucchini and Yellow Squashes

Although freeze-dried vegetables have been on the market for some time, their expense has inhibited many crafters from using them. Microwaved slices of these vegetables are pretty enough to use in natural wreaths, and take just a few minutes to prepare. First slice the squashes in 1/8-inch slices and arrange them in the microwave between two paper towels. Microwave on 50% power for 6 minutes, stopping halfway to turn them over. Add more time if needed in 2-minute intervals.

Pears

Prepare pears for microwaving as you would apples.

Melon and Squash Seeds

Crafters who make seed jewelry have often been frustrated with the amount of time it takes to dry the seeds. With the microwave, though, it takes just a few minutes. First remove the flesh from the seeds and soak them in a mixture of 1/2 cup bleach to 1 quart of water for 20 minutes. Rinse the seeds and pat off any excess moisture. Place a single layer of seeds between two paper towels and microwave them on 50% power for 5 minutes, turning halfway during the drying time. Check for dryness and add extra time in 90-second intervals if necessary.

Okra

Okra adds interesting color and shape to arrangements and wreaths. They shrivel up too much when completely dried in the microwave, so remove them when halfway dry and allow them to air dry. First make several holes in both ends of the okra with a fork. Microwave on 50% power between two paper towels for 3 minutes or until they just begin to shrivel.

Flowers and Herbs

Successful flower and herb drying in the microwave depends as much on luck as it does on skill. Yes, certain types of blooms and foliage tend to do well, but even those can't be counted on 100%. Several factors influence the appropriate microwaving times and how well the finished blooms will look. These factors include: what stage of the blooming cycle the plant was in when it was harvested; how much moisture was in the plant (never harvest after a rain storm or early in the morning when there's still dew); the size of the blooms; the thickness of individual bloom petals; and the number of blooms being dried at one time. For these reasons, in addition

to the variations in microwave wattages, there are no hard and fast time guidelines for individual flowers and herbs. Instead, you'll need to start with a low time and wattage (1-1/2 minutes on 50% power) and add extra time in short increments. Blooms and foliage that usually air-dry quickly with little shrinkage (such as globe amaranth, strawflowers, and statices) will need considerably less time than most other blooms. Keeping a notebook filled with detailed success and failure notes can save you a lot of frustration in the future.

Flowers and herbs that work well are included in the list that follows. Unless otherwise indicated, the materials can be dried in a paper bag as directed on page 11 or between a few layers of paper towels. Mimosa, roses, coneflowers (silica gel), pin cushion flowers (silica gel), goldenrod, marigolds, calendula, tulips (silica gel), veronica, pansies (silica gel), poppies (silica gel) bee balm blooms, yarrow, hollyhock, dill, chamomile, feverfew, bachelor's buttons, astilbe, daisies, cosmos (silica gel), larkspur, snapdragons, cardinal flowers, alyssum, dahlias, lamb's ear foliage, mints, chervil, sage, fennel, coriander, thyme, marjoram, statices, strawflowers, globe amaranth, foxglove, heath, fuchsia, day lilies (silica gel), hydrangea, St. John's wort, ivy, pennyroyal, baby's breath, zinnias (silica gel), lemon balm, lemon verbena, basil, catnip, carnations, rosemary, santolina, snapdragons, and tarragon.

Moss and Fungi

Why would anyone want to put moss in their microwave, you may ask in bewilderment? Bugs, bugs, and more bugs, is the unfortunate answer. The moss that looked perfectly clean and innocent when you found it may in fact be filled with lots of tiny insects who would just love to move into your home.

Moss

To prevent unwelcome visitors, place the moss in a brown paper bag, gently fold up the ends, and microwave on 50% power for 15 minutes. To add color to the moss, prepare a spritz bottle with water and green food coloring and spray the moss with a light coating of the mixture after microwaving.

Fungi

Not everyone's favorite idea of a craft material, fungi add a natural look to wreaths, arrangements, and much more. Like mosses, though, they can carry hoards of small insects. To microwave,

arrange the fungus between a layer of paper towels and microwave on 50% power for 6 to 10 minutes, depending on the size and number of materials.

Cones, Pods, Seedheads, and Nuts

Like mosses, microwaving these materials can prevent small bugs and insects from infesting your craft

materials. Microwaving also offers several additional benefits, such as opening up the petals of cones and drawing up the meat in nuts for easy removal.

Cones

Place four or five cones in a paper bag and microwave on 50% power for 8 to 10 minutes. For cones that were harvested with their petals closed, add extra time in 3-minute intervals until the petals open.

Pods and Seedheads

Microwave 7 to 12 items in a brown bag for 8 to 10 minutes to kill any larvae and open up any contracted pods.

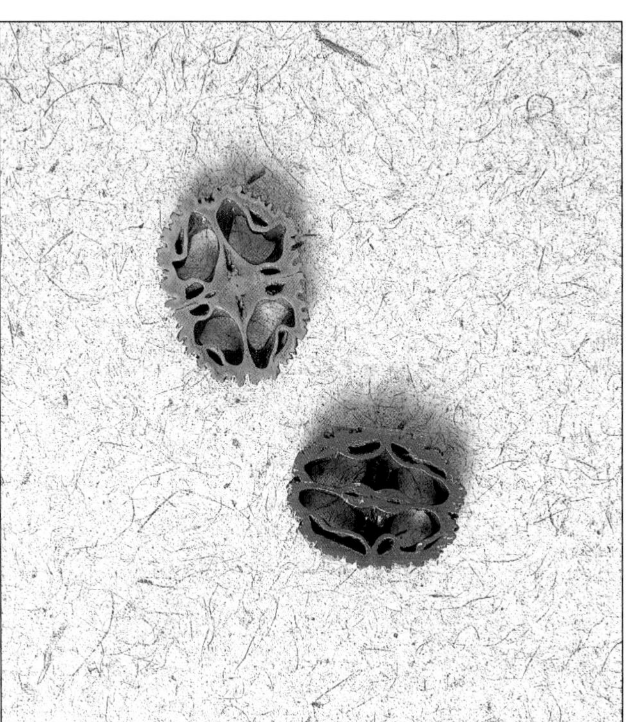

Nuts

Place a walnut (or other decorative nut) in a vise and make 1/4-inch slices. Place the sliced nuts between paper towels and microwave on 50% power for 3 minutes. The nuts are ready when the meat has dried out and drawn up, making it easily removed with a fork prong. Add extra time if needed in 1-minute intervals.

Disappointments and Disasters

Discovering and celebrating microwave success stories is great fun, but perhaps equally valuable is knowing what doesn't' work in the microwave. Following is a list of natural materials to avoid — unless of course you have an untamable crafter's imagination and don't mind cleaning out some nasty messes from your microwave while you explain to family and friends why your kitchen smells so awful.

Pomegranates (they ooze as they cook); Berries (they explode — yikes, what a mess); star fruit (they burn long before they dry); grapes (yes, they dry to raisins, but raisins aren't renowned for their craft potential); many spring flowers, such as lilies (they turn brown and wither); lavender (the notable fragrance evaporates); chive blooms (they shrivel and lose their fluffy shape); red onion slices (the spirals unroll and the odor is abominable).

Flowers Herbs and Sundries

Snowflake Tree Centerpiece

Hydrangea blooms, often referred to as snowballs for their color and fluffy shape, dry well in the microwave. This centerpiece adds an elegant, festive look to any table and takes less than an hour to make.

■

Materials

12-inch (30 cm) paper or silk pine tree with base, 8 dried hydrangea heads broken into clusters, narrow white ribbon, 2 white silk birds, gold glitter spray paint

■

Instructions
Designer Tips

Beginning at the base of the tree, spread the branches and tilt their tips slightly upward. Hot-glue the blooms between the branches in layers, beginning at the bottom and working around and up to the top of the tree.

Starting at the top of the tree, begin looping the white ribbon down and around the tree, hot-gluing as needed for reinforcement. Hot-glue the birds at the top and the bottom of the tree to cover the raw ribbon ends. Spray the entire tree with a light layer of gold glitter paint; repeat once or twice more if a more heavily gilded effect is desired.

Doily Delights

These decorated doilies can be used as hostess gifts, tree ornaments, place settings, package decorations, or just to add a bit of floral color to a shelf of knickknacks. The roses were dried in a brown paper bag over a bowl on 50% power in the microwave.

■

Materials

Cotton doily,
narrow satin ribbon,
fabric stiffener,
dried flowers, glue gun

■

Instructions
Designer Tips

Dip the doily in stiffener and fold the sides over to form the bouquet holder. For a smaller doily, you may want to roll the top edges back, pinning them in place until dry, as shown in the photo. Arrange the stems of materials at different depths in the holders and glue their stems in place. Tie the ribbon into a multi-loop bow and glue it to the outside of the bouquet holder. Trim with a whole bloom near the bow if desired.

Another way to decorate doilies is to cut them in half, dip them in stiffener, and gather them on their flat edge into a fan shape. Glue a multi-loop bow on the bottom edge, then trim with whole flowers and blooms.

Rose Basket

For your next gift-giving occasion, consider placing the gift in a floral basket instead of in wrapping paper. The basket is simple to decorate, and the cost is virtually the same as buying some fancy paper and ribbon. The roses were dried in a brown paper bag over a bowl at 50% power in the microwave.

Materials

Small basket with lid, lace, moss, dried roses and baby's breath, glue gun

Instructions / Designer Tips

Cut two lengths of lace that are double the distance around the outside of the basket's lid. Gather one strip of the lace to fit the lid and hot-glue in place, then repeat with the second strip of lace. Cover the remaining surface area with moss, and glue the flowers into the moss. Decorate the basket's body by hot-gluing a length of lace around the center.

Ribbon Tieback

More delicate than the tiebacks in this chapter, this garland of flowers is so simple and inexpensive to make that it may solve many of your gift-giving dilemmas. The roses and wild flowers were dried in a brown paper bag placed over a bowl on 50% power in the microwave.

■

Materials

1/2-inch (12 mm) satin ribbon, dried flower blooms, moss

■

Instructions Designer Tips

Tie a length of ribbon around your curtain, mark the area that covers the front of the curtain with pins, and cut it to the correct length. Glue small pieces of moss to the area you marked with pins, then glue blooms into the moss. Trim away any unruly sprigs of moss with scissors.

Rose Trellis

Inexpensive vine bases make a lovely backdrop for displaying summer garden treasures. The designer added to the wreath's natural appeal by choosing roses in an assortment of sizes and growth cycles.

Materials

6-inch (15 cm) vine wreath base, rose blooms, buds, and foliage, glue gun, clear acrylic spray

Instructions
Designer Tips

Remove the foliage from the blooms and microwave them separately. Arrange and hot-glue the leaves on two sides of the wreath. Spray them with a light coat of clear acrylic spray, then hot-glue the roses in place.

Soothing Mint Tea

If you've never planted mint before, you may find the idea of drying the leaves in bulk for tea as far-fetched. But as any mint grower can tell you, just one small, innocent-looking plant will become a hedge of mint that's determined to take over your entire yard, so there will definitely be enough leaves for tea.

Materials

Any variety of mint leaves (orange mint, peppermint, spearmint, lime mint, chocolate mint, etc.), fusible tea bags (optional)

Instructions
Designer Tips

Spread the leaves over a microwavable paper towel and cook in the microwave until almost dry. Place them in an area free from moisture and allow them to finish drying. Store the leaves in a decorative, air-tight container for a nice gift or iron them into fusible tea bags (available in health and herbal supply stores).

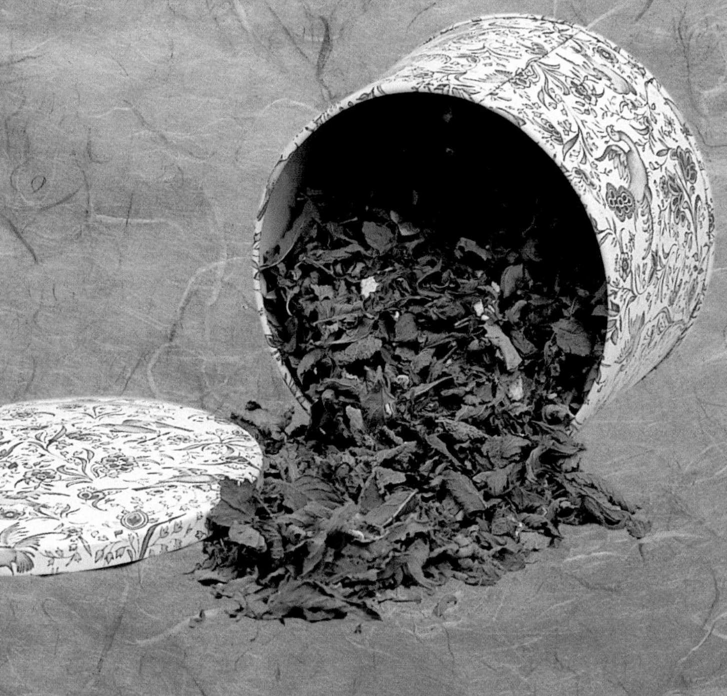

Blueberry Hill Potpourri

Although the fragrance of this potpourri comes from a synthetic essential oil, the beautiful colors and shapes of the natural materials make this potpourri a natural stand-out. Many of the materials — the celosia, oak moss, cones, annual statice, red rose petals, and rosemary — were dried in the microwave.

■

Materials

Pink crested celosia pieces, rose hips, red rose petals, oak moss, birch or hemlock cones, star anise, cinnamon chips, hibiscus, blue juniper berries, white annual statice, whole allspice berries, whole cloves, rosemary needles, ground orris root, blueberry essential oil

■

Instructions

Designer Tips

Mix the orris root and two teaspoons of the essential oil in a glass jar. Cover and let stand for five days, shaking the jar each day. Place the remaining potpourri ingredients in a plastic container with a tight-fitting lid. Add the mixture to the potpourri and shake well. Cover and let the fragrance cure for at least two weeks.

For best results, always buy the most expensive essential oil you can afford. (The fragrance from the cheaper oils can wear on your nerves after a day or two.) Be sure to use a plastic spoon for stirring a potpourri — not a metal one — to prevent the essential oil from spoiling when it comes in contact with the metal.

Teardrop Wreath

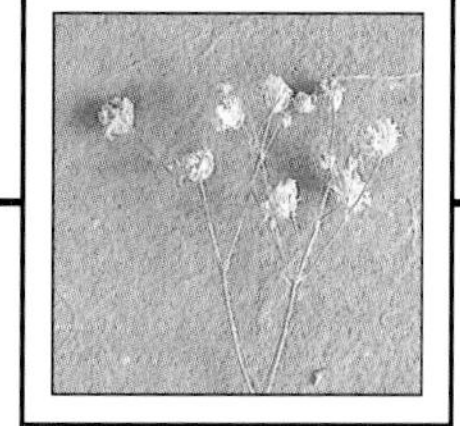

Sprigs of baby's breath, caspia, and ti tree, dried in the microwave, add a lacy, delicate look to this fragrant eucalyptus wreath.

■

Materials

Glue gun, pruning shears, 3-inch (7.5 cm) wooden floral picks, medium-gauge floral wire, vine wreath base, wired paper ribbon cord, eucalyptus, dried baby's breath, caspia, ti tree

■

Instructions

Designer Tips

Cut the eucalyptus into 6-inch (15 cm) lengths. Attach the eucalyptus to floral picks, two or three stems per pick. Squeeze a drop of hot glue onto the point of each pick and insert it into the base vines. Hot-glue single stems of eucalyptus in any bare areas. Tie the ribbon cord into a bow and attach it to the wreath with a short length of floral wire. Wind additional ribbon through the eucalyptus, securing it in three or four places with hot glue, then glue in pieces of baby's breath, caspia, and ti tree.

Daffodil Delight

With microwave drying, it's easy to preserve daffodils and other sweet symbols of spring's arrival, and to enjoy them in craft projects.

Materials

Vine wreath base, daffodils, pearly everlasting, strawflowers, globe amaranth, heather, glue gun

Instructions
Designer Tips

Dry the flowers in a paper bag as directed on page 18. Divide your daffodils into three piles and hot-glue them to the wreath base. Next, apply a dab of hot glue to the end of the heather stems and insert them into the vine. Last, cover the daffodil and heather stems with the remaining blooms, allowing portions of the vine base to remain exposed.

Herbal Teas

Fresh-blended teas are indescribably better than anything you can purchase at the grocery store, and they're a snap to make in the microwave. Chamomile blooms, scented geraniums, mints, lemon grass, lemon verbena, lemon balm, and sage all make nice teas, and you'll have great fun experimenting with different herb combinations.

Materials

Herb or herbs of your choice, fusible tea bags (sold in health food stores) or tea strainer

Instructions

Designer Tips

Arrange the fresh-cut stems of herbs on a paper towel and microwave at full power for one minute. Microwave again if needed in one-minute bursts at 50% power to prevent over-drying. Crush the leaves and place a teaspoon of them in the middle of a tea bag. Iron the edges closed as directed by the manufacturer.

Shadow Pictures

Shadow box frames are a wonderful way to display flowers from a wedding bouquet or other special occasion. The flowers can be arranged in a freeform bouquet or as they would be found in nature.

■

Materials

Shadow box frame set, clear-drying glue, dried flowers

■

Instructions

Designer Tips

Trace the shape of your frame area onto a blank piece of paper, and play with the arrangement of the flowers until you're happy with the results. Loosely outline their shapes so you'll have a placement guide to refer to as you work. Apply dabs of glue to the backs of the stems and blooms only in surface areas where they lie flat and press gently in place. When it comes to glue, less is definitely better, so use the bare minimum amount.

R ows of rosebuds and pearly everlasting are a wonderful way to encircle a special someone's photograph. This project also makes a fast, fun way to rejuvenate old picture frames.

■

Materials

Wood or mat picture frame, rosebuds, glue gun

■

Instructions Designer Tips

Dry the rosebuds and pearly everlasting as directed on page 18. Hot-glue several rows of blooms around the photo opening, following the opening's shape or creating your own.

Rosebud Frame

Herbal Folly

The whimsical curves of santolina (also known as lavender cotton) help create the simple beauty of this herbal wreath. The wreath does not require a large quantity of materials and looks as nice on a 10-inch base as it does on a 25-inch base. The large roses, bee balm, and carnations were all dried in the microwave with silica gel.

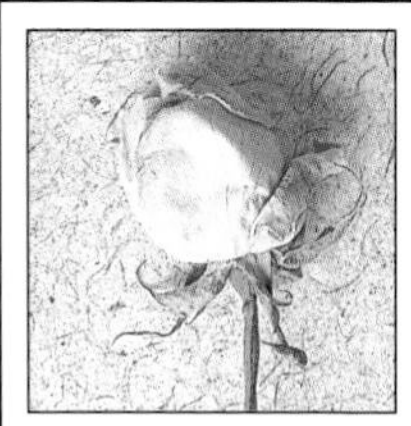

Materials

Dried roses (buds and open blooms), bee balm, carnations, santolina, moss-covered base, floral picks, glue gun

Instructions Designer Tips

Attach short stems of santolina to floral picks and insert them around the base to create a background for the blooms. A little moss showing through the santolina looks nice. Position the large rose blooms evenly around the wreath and hot-glue them in place. Then hot-glue a bee balm bloom on each side of the large roses, and fill in the areas between the roses with carnations and miniature rose buds.

Glimmering Wreath

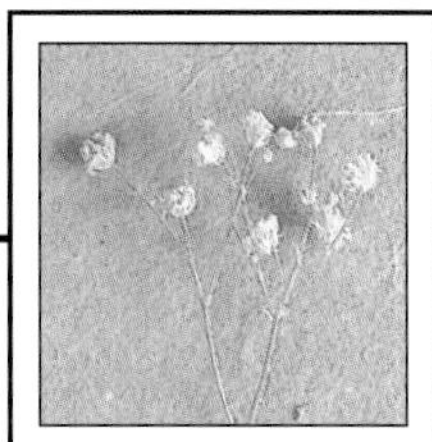

This gilded wreath is festive enough for the winter holiday season but also lovely enough to grace a bedroom year 'round. The baby's breath, statice, and feverfew were dried in the microwave, while the Spanish moss was gathered fresh and then zapped to kill any unwelcome pests.

■

Materials

16-inch (41 cm) foam wreath base, Spanish moss, floral pins, glue gun, narrow gold wired ribbon, baby's breath, feverfew, white annual statice, canella berries, love-in-a-mist pods

■

Instructions Designer Tips

Create a good adhesion surface by covering the base with Spanish moss using the floral pins. Break the branches of canella berries into small stems and hot-glue them around the wreath. Next, hot-glue the baby's breath, the statice, and the feverfew blooms around the wreath.

Gently wrap the gold wired ribbon around the wreath, forming bow loops at the top if desired. Last, gently hot-glue the delicate love-in-a-mist pods around the wreath.

Almost everything benefits from a little embellishment with dried flowers, even this needlepoint fan. The feverfew, rose buds, daisies, and larkspur were all dried in the microwave.

Materials

Fan, narrow ribbon, narrow lace, glue gun, feverfew, rose buds, daisies, larkspur

Instructions

Designer Tips

Arrange the floral materials together in a small bouquet and tie them together with the lace. Place a dab of glue on the lace on the back side of the bouquet and press it in place on the fan. Hot-glue five or six narrow ribbon streamers to the back side of the fan, and then finish by hot-gluing a rose bud to the end of each ribbon.

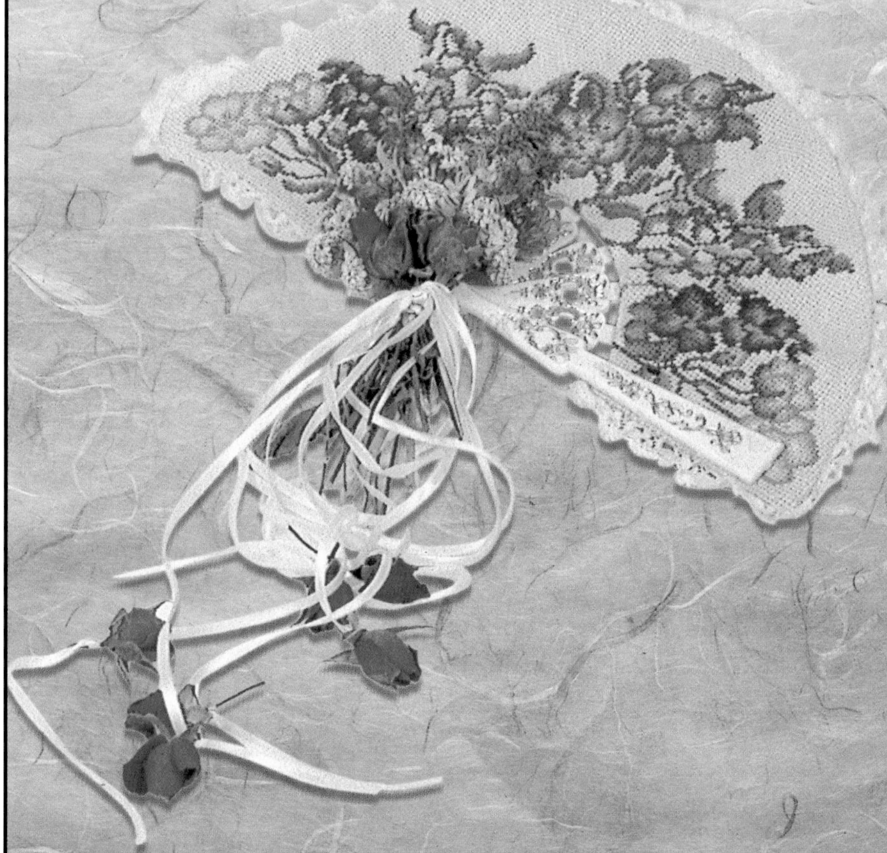

Floral Fan

This fragrant ornament creates a Victorian mood on a holiday tree. After the holidays, hang it over a doorknob or bedpost for year-round enjoyment.

■

Materials

Lace, tulle, narrow satin ribbon, floral wire, potpourri, dried whole blooms, (strawflowers and globe amaranths were used here), glue gun.

■

Instructions

Designer Tips

Using a salad plate as a pattern, cut out a circle of lace and a circle of tulle. Cut out a coin-size hole in the center of both fabrics and stitch a row of gathering stitches around the outside of the holes. Cut out a 4-inch (10 cm) square of lace and place a tablespoon of potpourri in the center. Gather up the outsides, twist, and secure with floral wire to form a small sachet.

With right sides facing up, place the tulle circle on top of the lace circle, lining up the center holes. Place the sachet on top of the lace and press the excess sachet fabric through the holes. Pull the gathering strings tight, tie them off, and secure the three layers together on the back side with a dab or two of hot glue. Hot-glue a hanger at the top of the ornament and ribbon streamers under the sachet, then hot-glue the whole blooms around the sachet.

Lace Tree Ornament

Cattail Wall Swag

This versatile swag can be displayed on a wall or placed on a dinner table for a beautiful centerpiece. If you can't find the cattails at a craft store, substitute some unusual looking twigs.

■

Materials

2-inch (5 cm) square of floral foam, floral wire, floral tape, glue gun, 30 - 40 cattails with long stems, larkspur, ti tree, poppy pods, ferns or other foliage, caspia, raffia, warm melt glue gun

■

Instructions

Designer Tips

Dry the larkspur, ti tree, caspia, and fern foliage in separate batches in the microwave on 50% power. Bundle up all the cattail stems and secure them together in the center with a length of floral wire that's been wrapped with floral tape. (The tape will prevent the wire from cutting into the delicate stems.) Form a hanger from a 4-inch (10 cm) length of floral wire and twist it in place around several cattail stems on their back side.

Glue the foam block to the center top of the cattail stems. Make a bow from the raffia and hot-glue it to the foam. Position the poppy pods around the bow and hot-glue them in place. Begin inserting the larkspur stems into the foam at different depths, then insert the ti tree stems. Fill in the bare areas with stems of caspia and fern.

Catnip Toys

These simple projects will provide hours of pleasure for you and your favorite feline. Catnip plants, if you can keep the cats away from them, are easy to grow. To dry the fresh-cut stems, place them in rows on a paper towel and microwave on high for one minute; turn the stems over and microwave for another minute. Add additional time in small increments at 50% power to prevent over-drying.

Materials

Scraps of burlap or other sturdy fabric, scraps of yarn, bells, dried catnip leaves

Instructions / Designer Tips

Strip the leaves from their stems and crumble them. For each toy, cut out two rectangles measuring 5 x 4 inches (13 x 10 cm). Place the rectangles together with wrong sides facing and topstitch three of the edges 1/2 inch (12 mm) in from the edges. Fill the toy with the crumbled catnip and topstitch the open edge closed. Pull three or four threads out on each edge to create a fringe effect, then hot-glue a bow and bell on top.

Decorated Basket

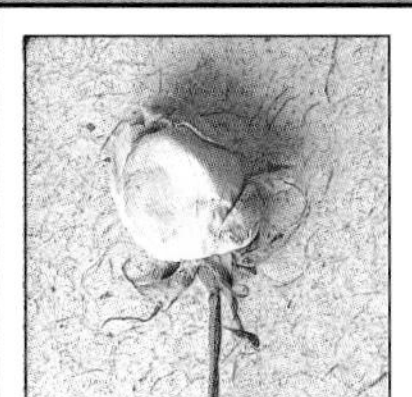

Subtle color variations in the materials decorating the basket's rim resonate between all the materials, making the silk berries a natural accompaniment to the dried flowers.

■

Materials

Basket, German statice, rose buds, decorative ribbon braid, stem of silk berries, glue gun

■

Instructions
Designer Tips

Dry the roses and German statice as directed on page 18. Cut the statice into 3-inch (7.5 cm) lengths and glue them around the rim of the basket, taking care to position all the stems in the same direction. Loop the braided cord around the basket, reinforcing as needed with dabs of hot glue. Space the rosebuds evenly around the basket and hot-glue them in place. Trim the stem of berries down into several shorter lengths and hot-glue them in place. Last, create a small arrangement at the top of the basket from statice and a few single berries.

Curtain Tiebacks

These curtain decorations are built on a base of paper greenery. The strawflowers, oregano blooms, baby's breath, larkspur, yarrow, and feverfew blooms were all dried in the microwave.

Materials

Paper or silk evergreen garland, glue gun, narrow ribbon, green floral wire, baby's breath, pearly everlasting, hops, strawflowers, yarrow, oregano blooms

Instructions
Designer Tips

Cut four 27-inch (67 cm) lengths of paper greenery from a garland. Secure the four lengths together at the top with a piece of green floral wire and braid them together (1 x 2 x 1). Curve the braided greenery into a circle and secure the ends with floral wire.

Cut two lengths of ribbon streamers, one measuring 46 inches (115 cm) and one measuring 33 inches (83 cm). Attach the streamers with floral wire to the side of the circle that will be next to the window frame. Tie a bow from the ribbon and wire it to the garland circle overlapping the ribbon streamers.

Working toward the bow from the opposite side, hot-glue a background of baby's breath to the greenery, keeping all of the stems facing in the same direction. Next, add blooms of larkspur, pearly everlasting, hops, strawflowers, yarrow, and oregano. Feel free to use whatever blooms you have available.

Oval Rose Wreath

Long revered for their natural beauty, fragrance, and symbolic meanings, roses are still a favorite choice for floral projects. Although roses can be temperamental when preserved with traditional air-drying techniques, they tend to dry remarkably well in the microwave.

■

Materials

11- x 13-inch (27 x 32 cm) oval vine base, silver king artemisia, rose buds and 5-inch (13 cm) stems of rose blooms and leaves, brown yarn, dried heather, glue gun

■

Instructions

Designer Tips

Dry the roses in the microwave as directed on page 18. Cut the artemisia to 6-inch (15 cm) lengths and arrange the stems in bouquets of four to six stems. Position the first bouquet against the top of the wreath and tie it on with yarn. Arrange the remaining bouquets with the stems facing in the same direction, positioning each new bouquet to cover the stems of the previous one. For a fluffier wreath, alternate the angle at which you place the artemisia bouquets, from left, to straight ahead, to right. Continue adding bouquets until the entire base is covered.

Trim the heather to 4 inches (10 cm) and gently insert it in pairs under the yarn from the artemisia bouquets. Finish by hot-gluing in the rose stems and single blooms.

Golden Rod Glory

Long the victim of rumors that it causes uncontrollable sneezing outbursts, goldenrod's name is finally being cleared by many allergists, so its beautiful colors and shapes can be enjoyed by gardeners and crafters alike.

■

Materials

Fresh-cut sweet Annie, goldenrod, dried blue salvia, dried rudbeckia, monofilament or raffia, glue gun

■

Instructions
Designer Tips

Group eight or nine 20-inch (50 cm) stems of sweet Annie together, curve them into a wreath shape, and secure the sweet Annie with wraps of monofilament or raffia in 2-inch (5 cm) intervals. Dry the goldenrod in the microwave as directed on page 40. Trim the goldenrod and blue salvia into 2-inch lengths and hot-glue them around the wreath, allowing their unusual curves to spill outside the wreath form. Last, hot-glue the rudbeckia blooms around the wreath.

Enchanted Birdhouse

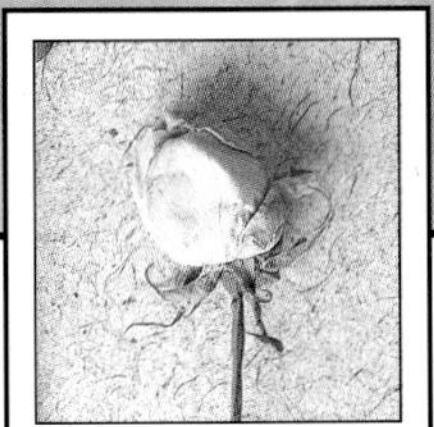

Microwaved flowers make just the right accents for a decorative indoor birdhouse. You can work with a purchased birdhouse or assemble and paint one from scratch.

■

Materials

Birdhouse, pearly everlasting, rosebuds, globe amaranth, yarrow, heather, goldenrod, glue gun

■

Instructions

Designer Tips

Microwave the blooms as directed on page 18. Hot-glue the blooms to the roof area, around the base, and in several smaller arrangements around the house. If you don't have a large supply of blooms, consider covering part of the house in sheet moss.

Square Wreath

This glimmering wreath is festive enough for the holidays, although it also looks nice in everyday use in a more formal home. The designer chose to turn a square wreath base on its diagonal and then emphasize the shape with ribbon curls.

■

Materials

13-inch (33 cm) square vine wreath base, floral wire, brown yarn, air-dried mint blooms, blue and pink larkspur, gold ribbon, decorative angel, glue gun.

■

Instructions
Designer Tips

Dry the larkspur in the microwave as directed on page 18. To form a hanger, insert a short length of floral wire through some of the top vines on the base's back side, form a loop, and securely twist the wire. Separate the dried materials into two large and two small bouquets of mint blooms, two bouquets of pink larkspur, and two bouquets of pink and purple larkspur mixed together. Position one of the large mint bouquets about halfway up each side of the base and tie them in place with yarn. Place a bouquet of pink larkspur next to the mint blooms, allowing for a little overlap, and tie them in place. Repeat on each side with a smaller bouquet of mint, then finish with the two-color larkspur bouquet. Reinforce the bouquets with hot-glue as you work.

Hot-glue two lengths of gold ribbon into the vine at the top of the base, twist them down the sides, and hot-glue their ends into the second bouquet of mint blooms. Hot-glue a large gold ribbon bow in the bottom center to cover the area where the stems meet, and then hot-glue the angel in the center of the bow. Last, cut two ribbon streamers and hot-glue them under the ribbon.

Bath Powder

Blending compatible fragrances of herbs and essential oils is the trick to special bath powders. Rose scented geranium leaves and rose oil, lavender blossoms and rose oil, and lemon verbena and lemon oil, all make good combinations, but you should feel free to experiment beyond these combinations.

■

Materials

1-1/2 cups cornstarch,

1/2 cup dried herbs,

30 drops of essential oil.

■

Instructions Designer Tips

Dry the herbs on a paper towel in a microwave at full power for one minute. Turn the stems over and add additional time in one-minute bursts at 50% power to prevent over-drying. Grind the herbs into a fine powder. Stir the herbs and the essential oil into the cornstarch powder until it's mixed well.

Bath Bags

Enjoy the fragrant and rejuvenating pleasures of an herbal bath with this simple project. Favorite herbs include rose and calendula blooms, and mint, scented geranium, lemon verbena, and fennel foliage.

■

Materials

1/2 cup dried herbs,
handkerchief or face cloth,
ribbon or yarn

■

Instructions
Designer Tips

Dry the herbs on a paper towel in a microwave at full power for one minute. Turn the stems over and add additional time in one-minute bursts at 50% power to prevent over drying. Crumble the herbs and place them in the center of the handkerchief or face cloth and tie the bag closed. Tie the bag over the water spout or submerge it in your bath water.

Basil Arch

The rich green, red, and ivory colors in this project contrast beautifully with the natural texture and color of the vine arch background.

Materials

Vine arch base, basil, feverfew, globe amaranth, wired ribbon, glue gun

Instructions / Designer Tips

Microwave the basil, feverfew, and globe amaranth in separate batches between layers of paper towels. Begin the arrangement by hot-gluing the basil to the vine base, then hot-glue the feverfew blooms onto the basil. Tie the ribbon into a bow and hot-glue it in the lower center. Finish by hot-gluing bright globe ama-

Soothing, fragrant, and extraordinarily inexpensive, these lip balms are a wonderful way to enjoy herbs. The recipe below will yield enough lip balm to provide you with an inventory of special gifts for holidays and birthdays. The leaves from comfrey, lavender, and bee balm, and the flowers from chamomile and calendula, all make nice balms.

Materials

1 ounce shredded beeswax, 1 ounce aloe vera oil, 1 pound jar of petroleum jelly, 20 drops of liquid vitamin E, 2 tablespoons witch hazel, 2 tablespoons dried herbs, cheesecloth

Instructions / Designer Tips

Heat the petroleum jelly until softened in a large, microwave-safe container with a top. Add the beeswax and the herbs to the container and continue heating in 1-minute intervals on 50% power until melted, stirring between each heating. Strain the herbs by pouring the liquid through two layers of cheesecloth. Stir in the aloe, vitamin E, and witch hazel, then pour into containers.

Note: Be sure to do all stirring with a wooden or plastic spoon — not a metal one — to prevent disflavoring the oil.

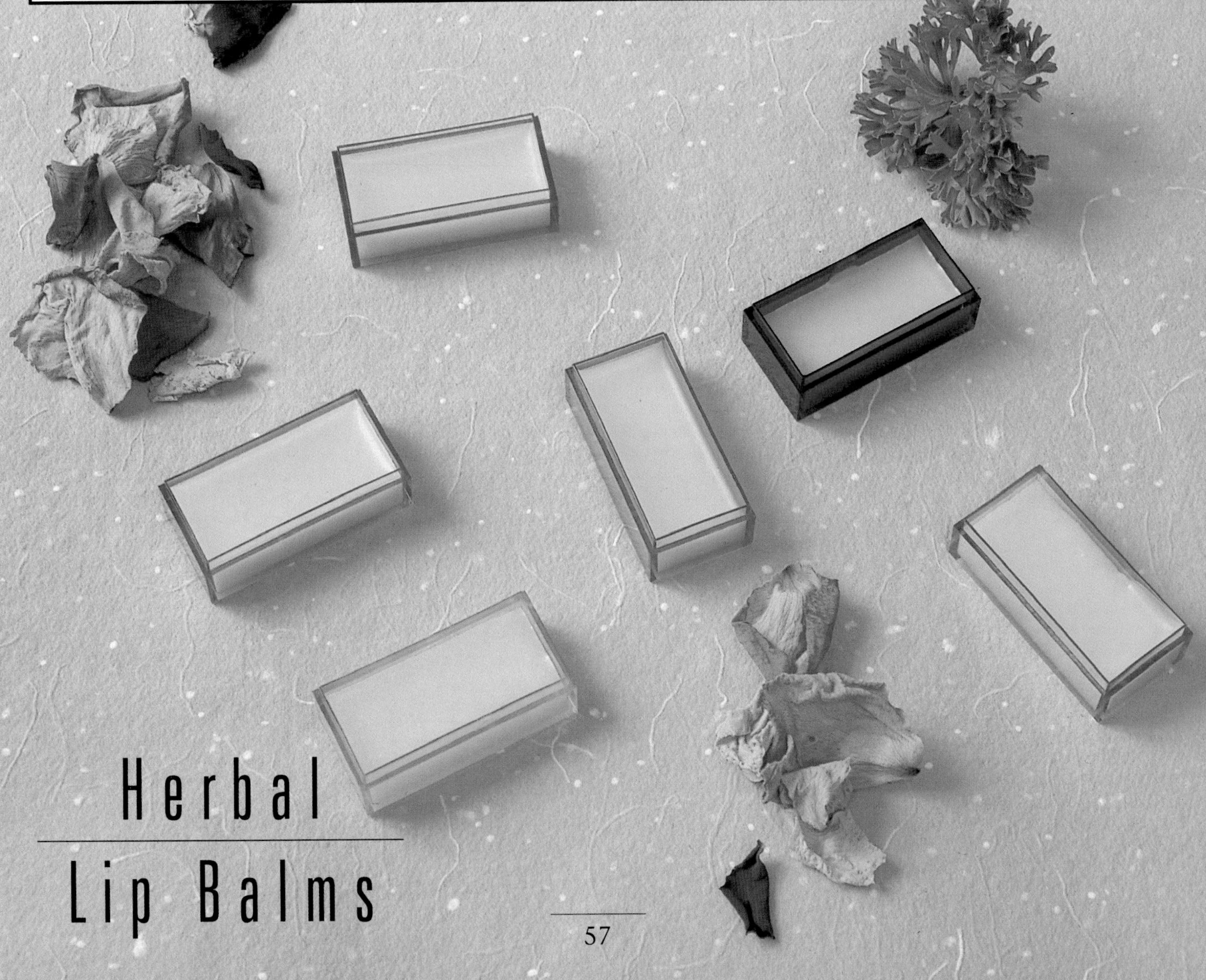

Herbal Lip Balms

Vine Heart

Decorating an inexpensive vine base with a spray of flowers and herbs creates a surprisingly simple yet beautiful wreath. The zinnia retained its color and shape when dried in the microwave with silica gel.

■

Materials

Small heart-shaped vine wreath base, dried dill, fennel, strawflowers, artemisia, zinnia

■

Instructions

Designer Tips

Dry the zinnia in the microwave in silica gel as directed on page 12. Cut the artemisia, the dill, and the fennel into 5-inch (12 cm) sprigs and arrange them in a spray with their stems facing the area where the vines overlap at the bottom of the heart base. Hot-glue them in place. Hot-glue a single strawflower bloom on each side, then hot-glue the zinnia in the center to cover the area where the stems meet.

Pansy Wall Hanging

The rich herbal fragrance emanating from this base of sweet Annie (botanically *artemisia annua*) adds an extra sensory dimension to the visual beauty of the pansies and other flowers.

Materials

Fresh-cut sweet Annie, purple and white annual statice, globe amaranth blooms, strawflowers, medium- and thin-gauge floral wire, glue gun

Instructions / Designer Tips

Dry the pansies in silica gel in the microwave as directed on page 12, and the annual statice, the globe amaranth, and the strawflowers as directed on page 18. From the medium-gauge wire, form an arched base measuring 7-1/2 x 11 inches (19 x 28 cm) with an X shape in the center. Trim the sweet Annie to 5-inch (13 cm) lengths and arrange it in bouquets of four to six stems each. Attach the stems of the bouquets to the base with the thin-gauge floral wire, taking care to position all bouquets in the same direction, with each new bouquet covering the stems of the previous bouquet. Hot-glue the flowers to the sweet Annie, saving the delicate pansies for last.

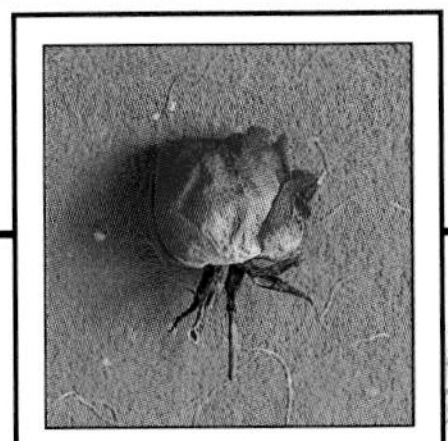

Whimsical raffia streamers arranged on a vine bow base with unusually shaped lemon mint blooms and bright red rosebuds creates a pleasantly original door or wall decoration.

■

Materials

Vine bow vase, tarragon, air-dried lemon mint blooms, rosebuds, wheat stems raffia, yarn

■

Instructions
Designer Tips

Microwave the tarragon and rosebuds as directed on page 18. Form two bouquets from the tarragon and the lemon mint blooms. Tie the bouquets together at the base of their stems with yarn, then tie them to the center of the vine base. Hot-glue the rosebuds and the wheat into each bouquet. Form loops of raffia by holding six or seven strands together and making figure-eights. Tie the loops to the vine with more raffia and reinforce with hot glue if needed.

Vine Bow

The stunning success of this wreath comes in part from the beautiful color complements created by the celosia's magenta, the off-white pearly everlasting, the mint's green and purple foliage, and the hydrangea, which features delicate strokes of all these colors.

■

Materials

16-inch (41 cm) heart-shaped straw wreath base, tulle, chenille stems or brown yarn, silver king artemisia, mountain mint, hydrangea, crested celosia, pearly everlasting, floral pins, floral picks, glue gun

■

Instructions
Designer Tips

Wrap the straw base with the tulle and secure it in place with several loose wraps of chenille stems or yarn. To form a hanger, bend a floral pin in half, insert it into the top back of the base, and secure with hot glue. Dry the hydrangea, celosia, and pearly everlasting in the microwave as directed on page 18.

Cover the inner and outer edges of the wreath base with small bunches of artemisia, using floral pins to anchor them securely in place. Position each new bunch of artemisia so that the blooms overlap the stems of the previous bunch. Pin small bunches of mountain mint foliage every few inches on top of the artemisia. Attach the hydrangea balls and small bouquets of pearly everlasting to floral picks and pick them into the center surface area. Finish by hot-gluing celosia blooms between the hydrangea and pearly everlasting.

Hydrangea Beauty

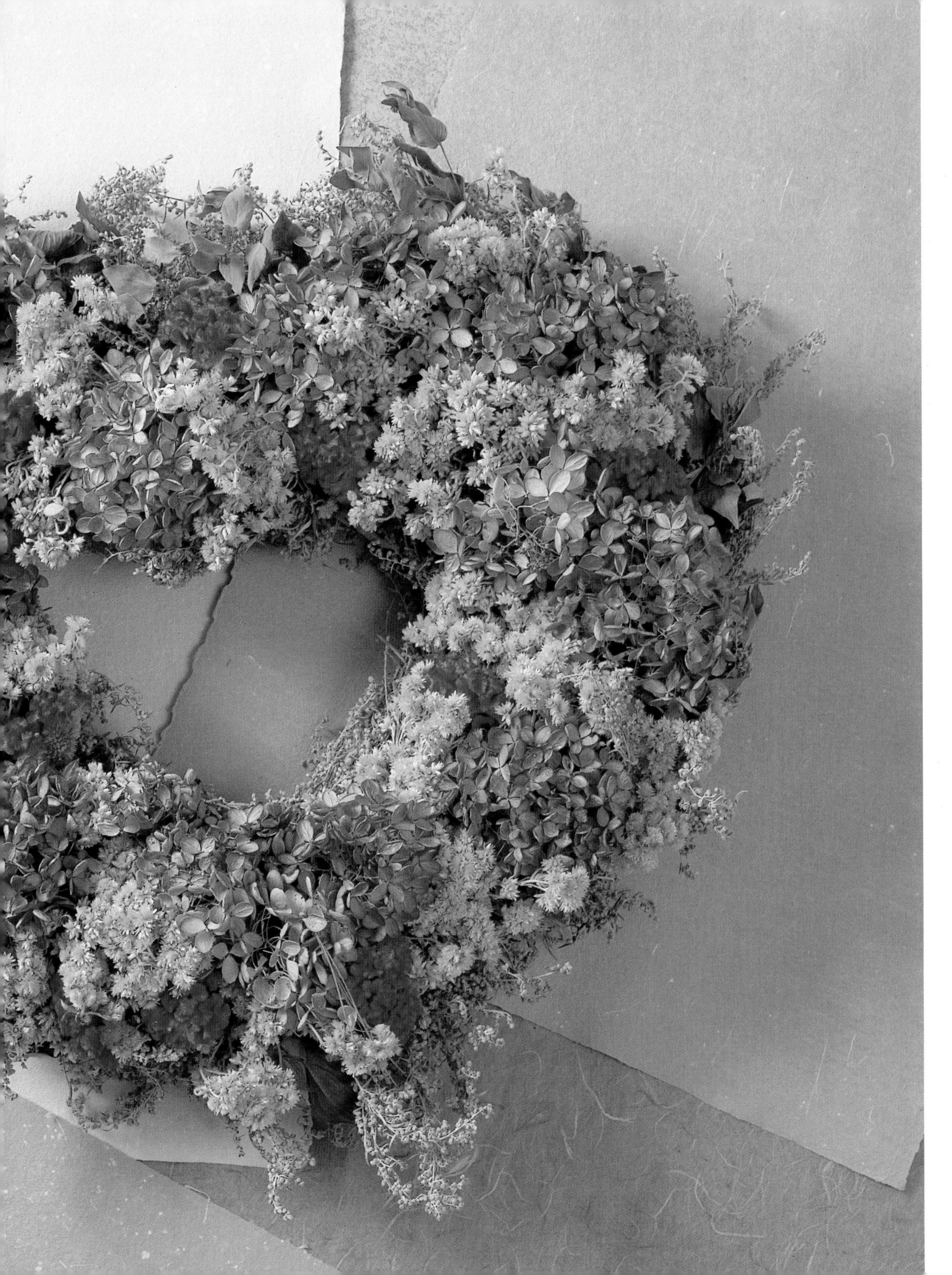

Birch Beauty

Although wreath bases rarely contribute to the finished look of a wreath, the rustic, whimsical look of the birch twig base is a major contributor to this wreath's success.

■

Materials

Twig wreath base, pink, white, and yellow yarrow blooms, strawflowers, globe amaranth blooms, neutral color of yarn, glue gun

■

Instructions

Designer Tips

Microwave the flowers as directed on page 18. Separate the flowers into bouquets containing a stem of each color of yarrow and a globe amaranth bloom, then trim the stems to 5 inches (13 cm). Tie the bouquets onto the base with the yarn, taking care to position all of them in the same direction with each new bouquet covering the stems of the previous bouquet. Last, hot-glue the strawflower blooms around the outside of the wreath.

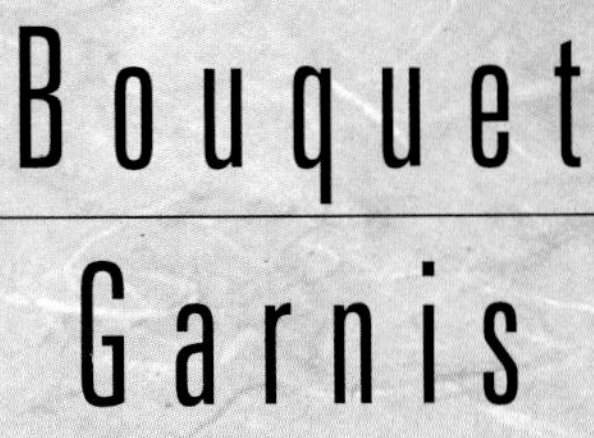

Bouquet Garnis

This pretty kitchen display of bouquet garnis can be disassembled for use whenever the flavor moves you. Good herb choices include basil, marjoram, thyme, borage, chervil, chives, coriander, dill, fennel, mints, rosemary, sage, salad burnet, tarragon, and lemon grass.

■

Materials

Small metal ring (for hanging), heavy ribbon, scraps of muslin, red peppers, assorted dried culinary herbs, needle and thread

■

Instructions

Designer Tips

Dry the herbs on a paper towel in the microwave for one minute at full power. Turn the stems over, then add additional time in one-minute bursts at 50% power. Insert one end of the ribbon through the ring, fold it down, and topstitch in place. Cut the muslin into 4-inch (10 cm) squares, and place the crumbled herbs in the center. Gather the sides up and loosely stitch the muslin to the ribbon. Continue adding muslin herb bags until you've reached the desired length. Loosely sew a hot pepper stem in between each bag. Crumbled culinary herbs can also be displayed in containers to be stored next to the stove.

Pet Collars

Filled with pennyroyal, which many herbalists believe to be a natural flea repellant, these flea collars provide attractive protection for beloved pets. Dry the pennyroyal stems in the microwave on a paper towel for one minute on full power, then add additional time if needed in small increments to prevent over- drying.

■

Materials

Scraps of cotton print fabric, sew-on Velcro strips, dried pennyroyal

■

Instructions

Designer Tips

Cut out a strip of fabric that's 2-1/2 inches wide x 4 inches longer (6 x 10-plus cm) than the distance around your pet's neck. Sew the long seam and one of the short seams with right sides facing and turn out. Cut the Velcro to a 2-inch (5 cm) length. Topstitch one of the Velcro sides on the sewn short edge. Stuff the tube with crumbled pennyroyal leaves, leaving about 2-1/2 inches unfilled. Fold the unsewn edge under 1/4 inch and topstitch the remaining length of Velcro in place. (*Note:* The Velcro strips should be sewn on opposite sides of the collar so that they will match up when the collar curves around the pet's neck.)

Moth-Repellant Sachets

Ancient herbalists recognized southernwood, tansy, and artemisia as an insect-repelling combination and they're still valued today.

■

Materials

Scraps of burlap or colorful fabric, southernwood, tansy, and artemisia foliage, lace appliqués (optional), ribbons, whole herb blooms or foliage, glue gun

■

Instructions

Designer Tips

Microwave the herbs on a paper towel on full power for one minute. Turn the stems over and add additional time in one-minute bursts on 50% power. Cut out two 4-inch (10 cm) squares for each sachet. If working with fabric, stitch all four edges together with right sides facing, leaving a small opening for turning. If working with burlap, topstitch three edges about 1/2 inch (12 mm) from the edge with the wrong sides facing. Crumble the dried herbs and place them inside the sachet, then whipstitch or topstitch the remaining opening closed. Decorate the outside of the sachet.

Pastel Wreath

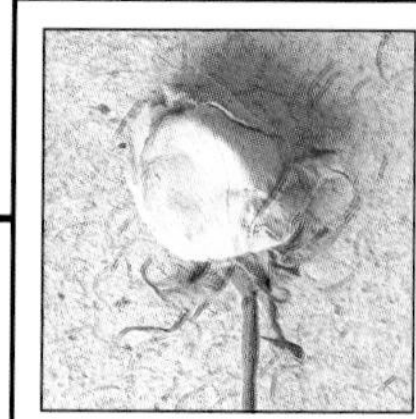

If you can't find a similar vine base, consider buying a natural vine base and applying color with a light coat of white or rose spray paint.

■

Materials

Vine wreath base, floral wire, larkspur, rosebuds, caspia, pepperberries, wired ribbon, glue gun.

■

Instructions

Designer Tips

Dry the larkspur, caspia, and rosebuds as directed on page 18. Arrange the caspia and larkspur into a bouquet and wire them together at the base of their stems. Arrange them on an angle against the wreath base and secure in place with hot glue.

Tie a length of wired ribbon into a bow and curve the streamers. Cut the bloom portion off several larkspur stems and hot-glue the stems under the bow to make the bouquet appear longer. Hot-glue single rose petals and stems of caspia under the bow, then create a small arrangement across from the bow of rose leaves, pepperberries, caspia, and a rosebud.

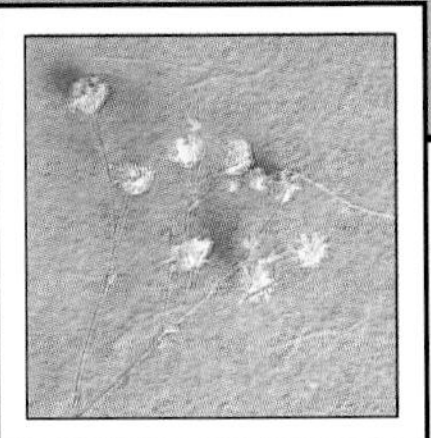

Ring in the winter holidays with this festive door decoration. The tips of the bells were decorated with whole cloves, adding a spicy fragrance to the project. The rosebuds and the baby's breath were dried separately in a brown paper bag over a bowl at 50% power. After the baby's breath dried, it was colored with a layer of red spray paint.

Materials

Sheet of 1-inch-thick (2.5 cm) foam, 4-inch (10 cm) length of medium-gauge floral wire, gold, red, and green wide-tip magic markers or acrylic paints, red spray paint, dried miniature and standard-size rosebuds, dried greenery, dried baby's breath, cloves, coriander seeds, glue gun

Instructions

Designer Tips

Enlarge the pattern on a photocopying machine to the desired size, and cut out the foam with a serrated knife. Fold the floral wire in half and insert the ends into the back of the foam to form a hanger, reinforcing with hot glue. Color in the areas to be decorated as indicated in the photo, then begin gluing on the miniature rosebuds and the cloves. Spray the baby's breath with a light coat of paint. With the tip of a pencil, press small holes into the foam, add a dab of glue inside the hole, and insert several stems of blooms. Glue the greenery in place the same way, then finish out the design with more rosebuds and the coriander seeds.

Jingle Bells

Fruits Cones and Intrigues

Herbal Garland

This lush garland makes a lovely, natural decoration for Christmas trees, although it also looks nice year 'round draped around a kitchen window. The orange and apple slices were dried in the microwave as directed on page 14.

■

Materials

Spool of 24-gauge wire, freeze-dried pomegranates, whole bay leaves, orange slices, apple slices, peanuts, cinnamon sticks, drill

■

Instructions

Designer Tips

Fit the drill with the smallest bit and drill holes through the centers of the pomegranates, the peanuts, and the cinnamon sticks. Cut one end of the spool wire at an angle so its pointed end will perforate the materials easily. Leave the wire on the spool for ease in handling the garland while it's being made.

Begin by threading 20 bay leaves onto the wire. Follow with five orange slices, then another 20 bay leaves, then five cinnamon sticks, then another 20 bay leaves, then a pomegranate, then another 20 bay leaves, then five peanuts, then another 20 bay leaves, then five apple slices. Add more materials in the order described above until you're happy with the garland's length.

Wearable Walnuts

Walnut slices make a surprising versatile decorating material. The jewelry pins, earrings, and barrettes take just a few minutes to make and can be colored with natural dyes for added effect if desired.

■

Materials

Walnuts, drill, hand saw, pin backings, earrings, barrette backings, glue gun, clear varnish.

■

Instructions
Designer Tips

Prepare the walnuts as directed in the basic instructions on page 19. For the pins and barrettes, hot-glue the walnut slices to the backings, then apply a coat of clear varnish. For the earrings, drill a small hole at the top of the walnut slices and slip the metal earring loop through it. Secure the loop with a pair of pliers, then apply a coat of clear varnish.

Citrus Braid

This wall hanging's refreshing citrus fragrance emanates from its base of braided lemon grass. If you don't happen to have a crop of lemon grass in your garden just waiting to be harvested, look for it in farmer's markets and health food stores.

■

Materials

40 - 50 stems of dried lemon grass, approximately 20 inches (50 cm) in length, floral wire, orange, lemon, and lime slices, cinnamon sticks, glue gun

■

Instructions
Designer Tips

Secure the stems of lemon grass together about 5 inches (12 cm) down from the top by twisting a short length of floral wire around them. Divide the stems into three equal portions and braid them until you're about 5 inches from the end. Secure the lower stems together as you did the top. Arrange and hot-glue the fruit slices down the braid, creating a flower-like arrangement of several layers in the center. Last, hot-glue a cinnamon stick under the fruit on each side.

Cinnamon Celebration

A lovely combination of fragrances, shapes, and colors contributed to the natural beauty of this wreath. If all of these materials aren't available, feel free to substitute other cones or fruit slices.

■

Materials

18-inch (46 cm) paper evergreen wreath base,
20 white pinecones,
60 apple slices,
14 pomegranates,
25 cinnamon sticks,
15 peanuts, 32 cedar cones,
Brazil and walnuts,
glue gun

■

Instructions
Designer Tips

Microwave the apple slices and the cones as directed on pages 14 and 19. Slice off the tops of the cedar cones to create the "roses." Hot-glue the pinecones around the outside, then follow with the pomegranates, the apple slices, cinnamon sticks, nuts, and cedar roses.

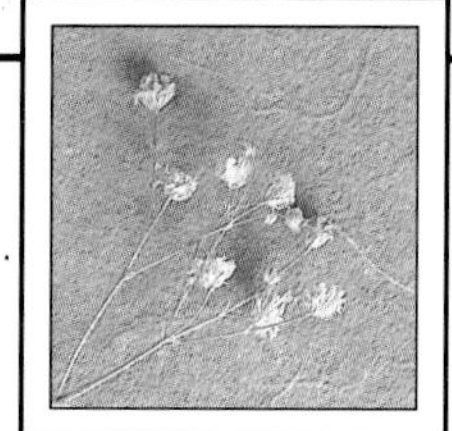

Stems of dried rosemary, arranged to look like sprawling evergreen trees, provide a lovely, woodsy fragrance. Although just a bird and squirrel were used here, any miniature forms could be arranged into the wreath.

Materials

10-inch (25 cm) grapevine wreath base with vine fence, rosemary, moss, miniature animals, pearly everlasting, pansies, globe amaranth, catnip, annual statice, Mexican mint, baby's breath

Instructions / Designer Tips

Microwave the moss, rosemary, and the blooms as directed on page 18. Hot-glue the moss around the bottom curve of the wreath base. Trim the rosemary to different lengths and hot-glue them around the fence. Fill in the remaining spaces with all of the blooms, then hot-glue the animals in place.

Note: If you can't find a twig wreath base with a built-in fence, a few minutes with a saw, a long twig, and a glue gun can create the same look.

Home Sweet Home

Decorated Pot

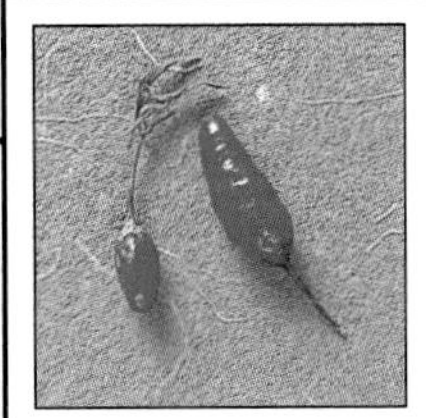

Slices of yellow squash and zucchini take on the look of expensive freeze-dried vegetables as they dry in the microwave. After decorating with vegetables, the pot can be filled with herbs, garlic bulbs, or other everyday cooking condiments.

Materials

Yellow squash, zucchini squash, bay leaves, chili peppers, ribbon, glue gun

Instructions Designer Tips

Microwave the squash and peppers as directed on page 16. Hot-glue the ribbon around the pot, then hot-glue the bay leaves to the ribbon. Arrange and hot-glue the yellow and green squash slices to the bay leaves, and finish by hot-gluing red peppers between the squash.

Apple Cinnamon Wreath

This small wreath looks nice near a spice rack or in virtually any other nook in the kitchen. It takes just a few minutes to make and the materials are refreshingly inexpensive.

■

Materials

6-inch (15 cm) foam wreath base, Spanish moss, apple slices, twine or raffia, cinnamon sticks, red wooden beads, glue gun

■

Instructions Designer Tips

Microwave the moss and the apple slices as directed on pages 18 and 14. Cover the base with moss and secure it in place by wrapping twine or raffia in 2-inch (5 cm) intervals. Attach the beads to a 20-inch (50 cm) length of twine or raffia, holding them in place with a knot on either side of them. Curve and loop the beaded twine around the wreath, securing with hot glue as needed. Hot-glue a twine bow to the moss, then hot-glue cinnamon sticks around and under the bow. Finish with the apple slices.

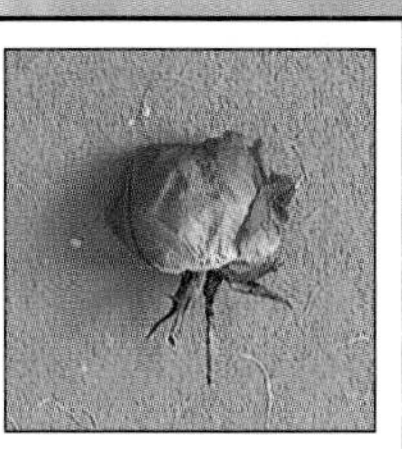

Winter Roses

The amazing color retention in the blooms and foliage of these roses makes them the perfect project for rose-lovers, enabling them to enjoy their blooms year 'round.

■

Materials

Small clay pot, foam ball, small stones, moss, rosebuds, caspia, decorative braided cord, glue gun

■

Instructions
Designer Tips

Dry the roses, caspia, and the moss in the microwave as directed on page 18, adding a spritz of color to the moss if desired. Fill the pot about halfway with the stones, place the ball in the center, and fill any excess space with more stones. Gently insert the rose stems into the foam ball. Drape the moss over the top of the ball and around the stems, allowing some to spill over the sides of the pot. Hot-glue several short stems of caspia at the base of the roses, then cover their insertion points with a single rosebud. Last, tie the decorative braid around the stems.

Gourd Bird

Gourd designers have a magical eye for seeing countless numbers of figures and forms in gourd shapes. The gourd in this project needed only a tail, beak, and legs to transform it into a bird.

■

Materials

2 gourds, wooden skewer, wood putty, piece of wood, sprigs of dried greenery, acrylic paints, drill, glue gun

■

Instructions
Designer Tips

Dry the gourds in the microwave as directed on page 15. Place one of the gourds on its side, mark the areas where you'd like the legs to protrude, and drill a hole through the gourd for each leg. Cut two 1-1/2-inch (4 cm) lengths from the skewer. Squirt some hot glue into the leg holes and insert the skewers. Mark the area on the wood where you'd like the bird to stand and drill a hole for each leg. Squirt some hot glue into each hole and insert the skewers. Drill three or four holes in the area where you'd like the greenery to appear and then glue the greenery in place as you did the skewers.

Form the claws for each foot with the wood putty. Mold the tip of the beak with putty and press in place. For the tail feathers, cut out a small half circle from the second gourd, curve the straight edge to fit the end of the gourd, and hot-glue in place. Paint the bird with several colors of acrylics, allowing some of the natural gourd color to show through if desired and taking care to paint over the wood putty areas.

These candle holders add a natural elegance to any room, and they fit in surprisingly well with just about any decor.

■

Materials

Glue gun, wooden pick, serrated knife, hemlock cones, two plastic or metal candle cups, polyurethane spray, 6-inch (15 cm) foam ball, two 6-inch diameter circles of green or brown felt, glycerin-preserved protea leaves, air-dried pearly everlasting, German statice

■

Instructions / Designer Tips

Microwave the cones in a brown paper bag as directed on page 19. Cut the foam ball in half with the serrated knife. Make a hole in the top center of each half ball wide and deep enough to accommodate the candle cup. Insert the cups. Starting at the top of the ball, hot-glue the cones around the candle cup opening. Continue gluing cones until the half ball is covered. Use the wooden pick to help secure each cone as it is glued in place by inserting the wooden tip along the bottom of the cone and applying gentle pressure. This process will also enable you to position them more closely together. Cover the second half ball with cones.

Spray the cones with polyurethane and allow them to dry. Carefully arrange and glue the protea leaves around the base of the sphere. Glue the felt circles to the bottom of the half balls. Hot-glue small sprigs of statice to each leaf in various positions, then hot-glue a red floral button at the center of each leaf where it meets the cones.

Safety Tip: Never leave the candles burning unattended, since the natural are flammable.

Hemlock Candle Holders

Gourd Tulips

Many varieties of small gourds are the perfect shape — with just a little cutting — for tulip flowers.

■

Materials

3 small gourds, 2 larger gourds for petals and pot (silk leaves and/or a clay pot can be substituted), 3 wooden skewers, green, red, and yellow acrylic paints, paintbrush, green floral tape, drill, glue gun

■

Instructions
Designer Tips

Dry the small gourds as directed on page 15. Cut off their tops, carve six petals in each one, and paint them red. Split the wood into several sections for about 1/4 inch (6 mm) on each skewer. Paint the split portion yellow (for the stamens) and the rest green (for the stems).

Insert the unsplit end of the skewers through the bottom hole until it protrudes in the tulip, then secure under the bloom with several wraps of floral tape.

For the pot, cut off the top of a larger dried gourd and drill several holes in the natural protrusion inside the gourd. Fill the holes with hot glue and then insert the tulip stems. Cut out the leaves from a larger dried gourd and insert them next to the tulip stems with the same technique used to adhere the stems.

Lamb's Ear Wreath

Notably named for the whisper-soft hairs on its foliage, lamb's ear leaves make a wonderful material for craft projects. The leaves tend to become brittle as they dry, though, so handle them carefully when removing from the microwave and arranging around a base.

■

Materials

Cardboard, lamb's ear leaves, strawflowers, money plant, narrow satin ribbon, glue gun

■

Instructions / Designer Tips

Microwave the lamb's ear leaves and the strawflowers as directed on page 19.

Create a wreath base by cutting out a 2-inch (5 cm) wide heart shape from the cardboard. Beginning at the bottom left, hot-glue the leaves to the cardboard. Stop when you reach the center top, then repeat the pattern on the other side. Hot-glue several leaves in a flowerette pattern at the center top of the wreath. Hot-glue the remaining materials in place.

Santolina Arch

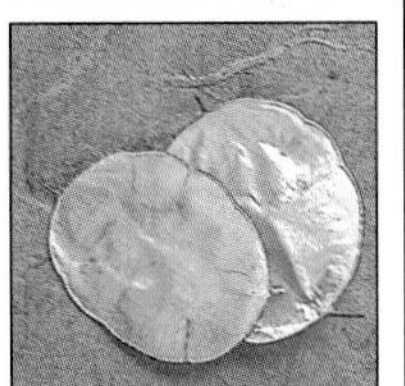

Also known as lavender cotton, santolina has long been appreciated by gardeners for the silvery color and whimsical shapes of its foliage. Santolina dries well in the microwave, and this makes an easy way to enjoy its beauty year 'round.

■

Materials

Grapevine arch, santolina, yarn, lion's ear or elephant garlic blooms, annual statice, Chinese lanterns, floral picks, glue gun

■

Instructions
Designer Tips

Microwave the santolina as directed on page 18. Cut the santolina into 4- to 5-inch (10 to 13 cm) sprigs and tie them to the base with their stems facing toward the center, beginning at each end and working inward. ends toward the center. Hot-glue additional sprigs in a starburst pattern as shown in the photo. Attach the lion's ear stems to floral picks and hot-glue the picks in place. Arrange and hot-glue the statice, then fill in the remaining spaces with the delicate Chinese lanterns.

Fabric Dyeing

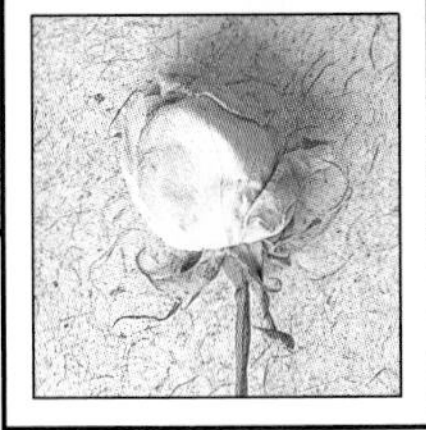

Bright dye baths are a snap to prepare in the microwave from fruits and vegetables, and they can be used to decorate any fabric whose fibers are 100% natural.

■

Materials

T-shirts, socks, scarves, place mats, or other fabric items to be dyed (100% cotton is recommended), making tape, newspaper, plastic wrap, sewing pins, dye applicator(s) (paint brush, string, sponges, spray bottle, etc.), prepared dye (see recipes on following page), potassium alum, cream of tartar

■

Instructions / Designer Tips

Cover a flat work surface with several protective layers of newspaper. Secure a layer of plastic wrap to the newspaper with masking tape. Pin the items you plan to dye through the plastic to the newspaper to keep them taut while applying dye.

To prepare the fabric to receive the dye, blend a mordant mixture of 2 tablespoons of cream of tarter and 8 tablespoons of potassium alum in one cup of water for each pound of fabric. Fill a large pan with water and blend the mordant in with it. Add the fabric, and add extra water to cover the fabric if necessary. Simmer for two hours on low heat (add extra time if brighter colors are desired), then remove the pan from heat and leave the fabric in the liquid for four to six hours. Rinse well and let dry. (Note: If you choose to skip this step, your beautifully dyed fabric will lose most of its color on its first laundering.

Apply the dye to the dried, mordant-treated fabric with the applicator(s) of your choice. Hang the fabric on a clothesline to dry, placing a layer of newspaper underneath the line to catch any drips if desired. Allow the fabric to completely dry, then let it sit for 24 hours. Hand wash the items in warm water, rinse, and hang dry. Subsequent washings can be done in the machine.

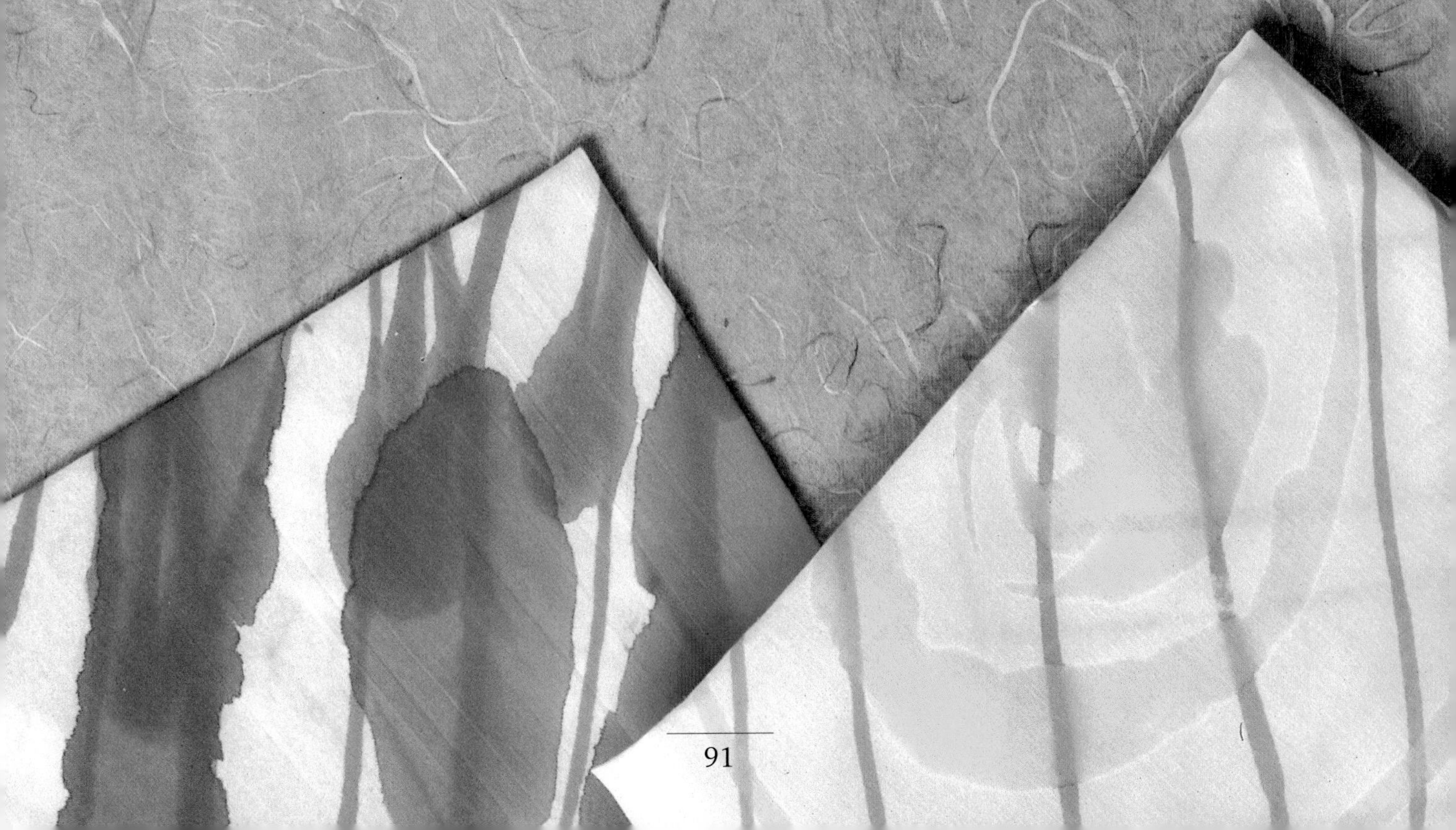

Color Dye Preparation

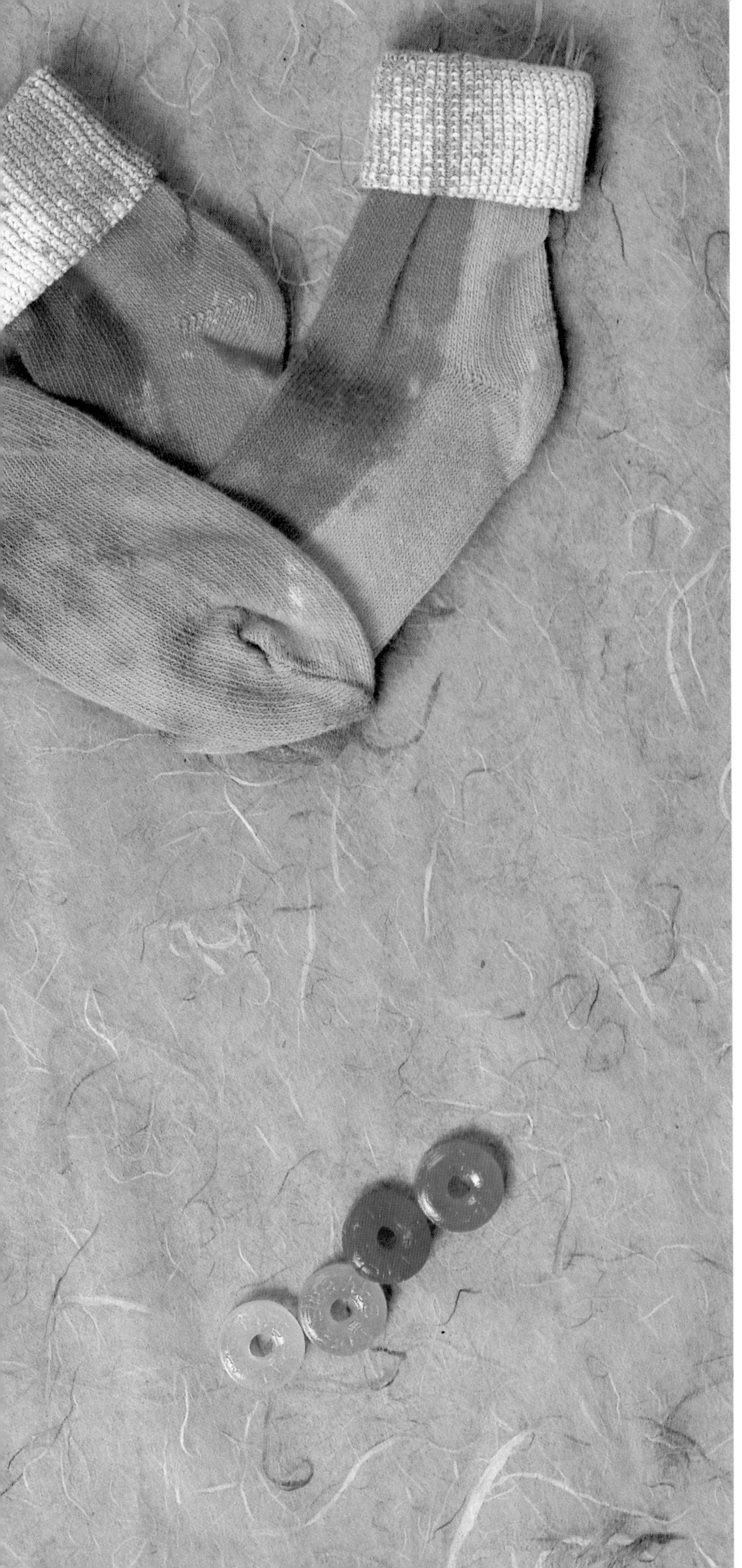

Red

Place 2 cups of fresh cranberries in a microwavable container and cover them with water. Microwave the cranberries on full power for five minutes (or until the mixture comes to a boil) with a paper towel over the top. Reduce the power setting to 50% power and microwave three more times in 3-minute blasts, stirring and crushing the berries in between each cooking cycle. When the berries are all crushed, stir one more time and microwave on full power for 3 minutes. Strain out the berries and save the liquid.

Blue

Chop a medium-sized head of read cabbage into strips and microwave it with 2 cups of water on 50% power for 20 minutes with a paper towel on top. Remove the cabbage from the microwave and stir, then microwave in two more 5-minute blasts, stirring in between each cooking cycle. Strain out the cabbage and save the liquid.

Yellow

Remove the outer skins from ten yellow onions and place them in a microwavable container with 2 cups of water. Cover the container with a paper towel and microwave on full power for five minutes. Remove the container, stir the onion mixture, and microwave for two more 3-minute blasts, stirring in between each cooking cycle. Strain out the onions and save the liquid.

Vine Wall Basket

Although silk and natural materials do not always work well together, the pleasing look in this project was achieved by arranging the materials so they appear to be growing out of a moss-filled basket.

■

Materials

Vine wall basket, stem of silk flowers, silk bird, moss, hydrangea, pepperberries, glue gun

■

Instructions

Designer Tips

Microwave the moss and the hydrangea as directed on page 18, adding a light spray of color to the moss if desired. Gently pack the moss into the basket. Press a pencil point into the moss, fill the holes with hot glue, and insert the hydrangea and pepperberry stems into the holes. Cut the stem of silk flowers into several shorter lengths and hot-glue them down into the moss, taking care not to damage the delicate hydrangea blooms and berries. Hot-glue the bird in place, then hot-glue a sprig of berries and hydrangea blooms to the top of the vine.

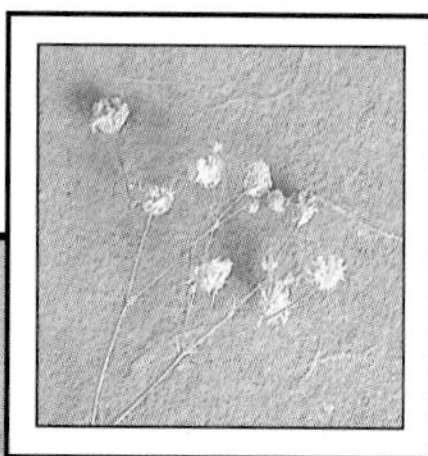

Culinary Wall Hanging

A vine wall basket makes a lovely base for this simple kitchen decoration. The moss and parsley were positioned with care to achieve a garden look.

■

Materials

Flat vine wall basket, moss, parsley, red peppers, garlic bulbs, glue gun.

■

Instructions / Designer Tips

Microwave the moss as directed on page 18 , adding a spritz of colored water if desired. Arrange the moss around the bottom portion of the basket and hot-glue it in place. Microwave the parsley as directed on page 18, then hot-glue the stems into the moss at natural angles. Hot-glue the hot peppers toward the center of the basket with their tips facing outward. Last, arrange and hot-glue the garlic bulbs to cover the pepper stems.

Seed Jewelry

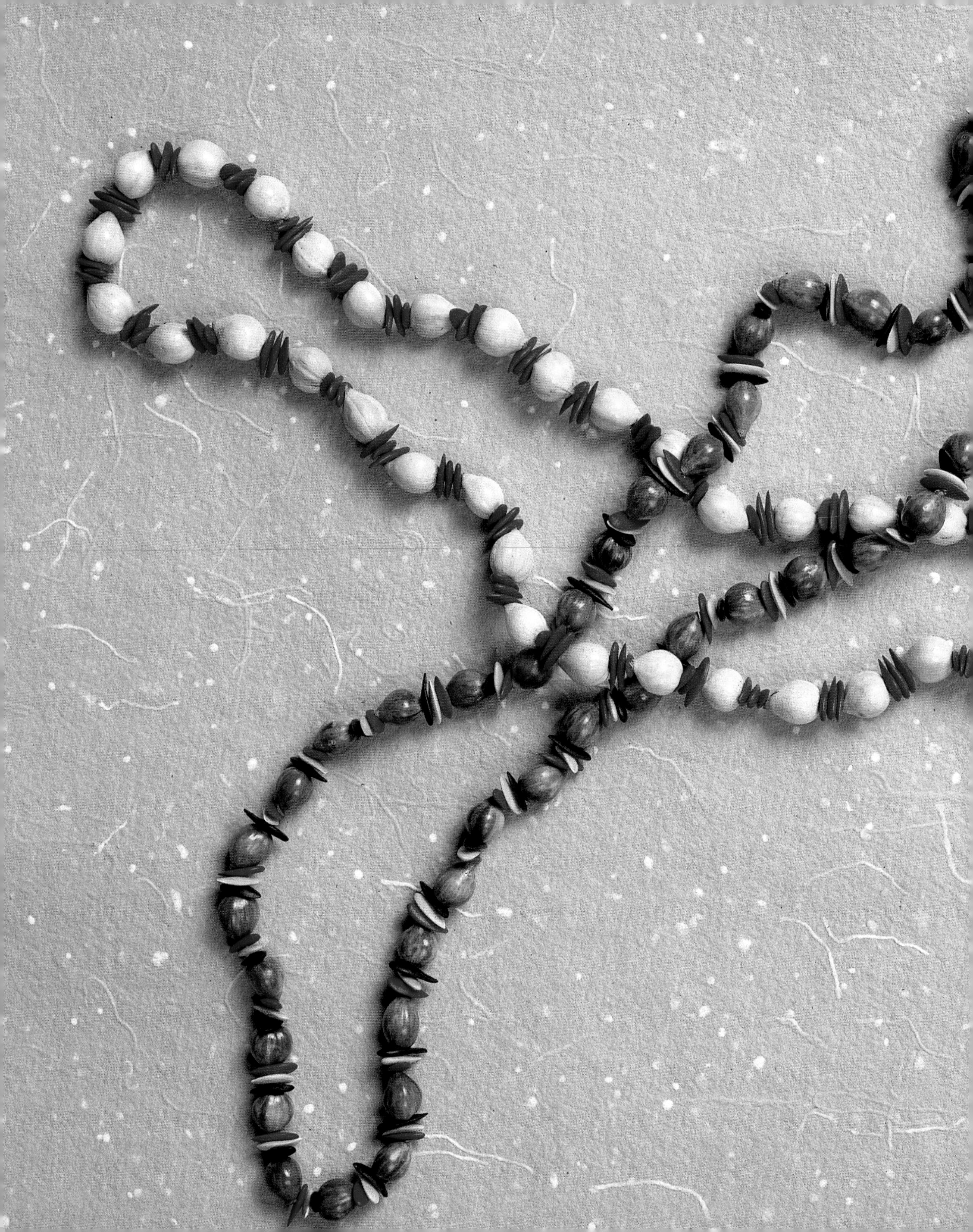

Seed Jewelry

Although the origins of seed jewelry can be traced back to early civilizations, it's surprisingly contemporary today. Seed jewelry is especially lovely when several varieties of seeds and a combination of colors — both dyed and natural — are used.

Materials

Pumpkin, cantaloupe, or gourd seeds, bleach, powdered fabric dye(s), strong thread, heavy sewing needle

Instructions
Designer Tips

Remove any flesh from the seeds and soak them in a mixture of 1/2 cup bleach to 1 quart water for 20 minutes. Rinse the seeds and pat off any excess liquid. Dry the seeds as directed on page 17. Prepare the dye as directed by the manufacturer and soak the seeds in it. Spread the seeds out on paper towels to dry, then string them with needle and thread. For easier threading, brace the needle with its eye end down against a hard surface, center a seed on top of the point, and press the seed down the needle.

Blooming Frames

Although few people think of Spanish moss as decorative in itself, it makes an especially nice material for framing antique photos. Note how well the ivy, which was dried in the microwave, retained its bright color and lovely foliage shape.

■

Materials

Mat frames, Spanish moss, foliage, blooms, glue gun

■

Instructions

Designer Tips

Microwave the moss, foliage, and blooms as directed on page 18. (Dahlias, ivy, and roses were used in the projects shown here.) Arrange and hot-glue the moss around one corner of the frame, then hot-glue the remaining materials into the moss. For an extra touch, you may want to create a small arrangement on the diagonal corner.

Wasp's Nest Wreath

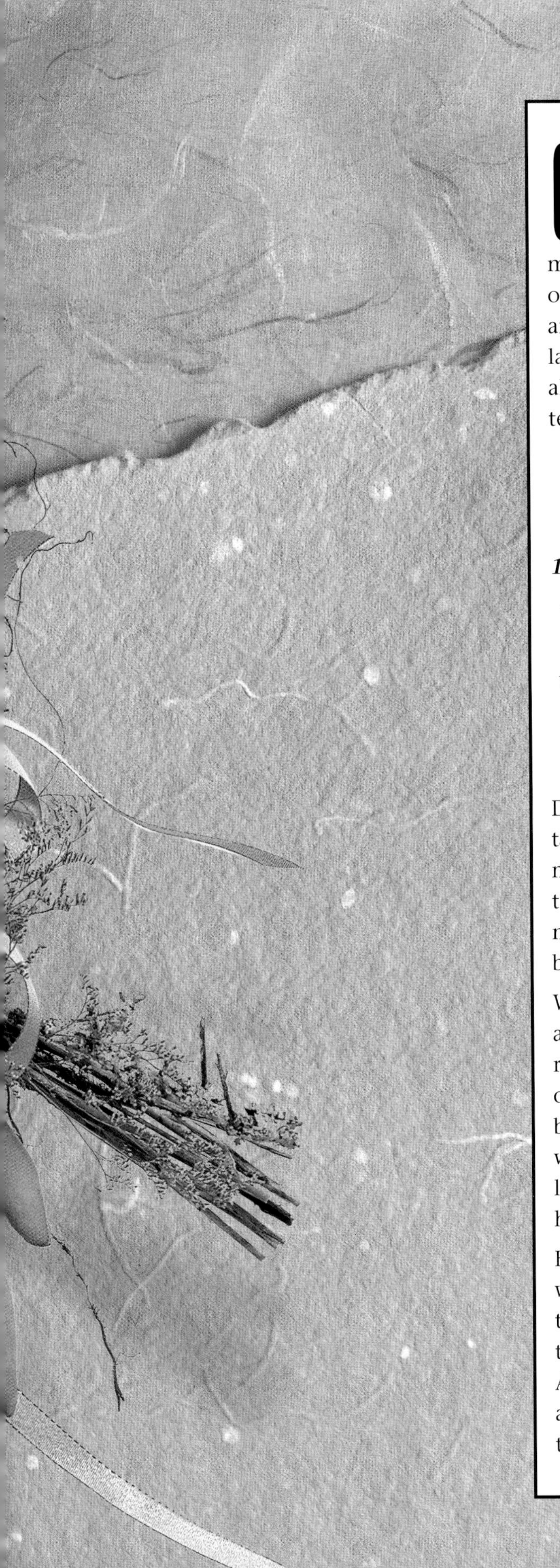

One of the few disadvantages to drying flowers in the microwave — you can't dry anything larger than what will fit on your microwave's turntable — can be overcome by creating an optical illusion or two. In this wreath, the large bouquet of larkspur (too large to fit in even the largest microwaves), is actually in two separate pieces, and the break is hidden under a protea bloom and a wasp's nest.

■

Materials

12-inch (30 cm) moss wreath base, floral wire, larkspur, small clumps of moss, several moss-covered twigs, globe amaranth blooms, rosebuds, caspia blooms, protea bloom, pieces of wasp's nest, two varieties of wired ribbon, silk pods, glue gun

■

Instructions / Designer Tips

Dry the fresh-cut larkspur stems in two batches: the first batch containing the blooms and as much of the stems as will fit in your microwave, and the second batch just the remaining stems. Dry the rosebuds, globe amaranth, and protea bloom in the microwave, then microwave the moss clumps and twigs in a brown bag to kill any insects.

Wire the larkspur blooms together at the very end of their stems and hot-glue to the base as close to the edge as possible, then repeat with the remaining stems together on the adjacent side. Cut one of the wired ribbon patterns into two lengths, hot-glue them between the larkspur stems, and curve them down each side of the wreath, hot-gluing as needed. Form loops in the remaining ribbon length, securing if needed with a short length of floral wire, and hot-glue between the larkspur stems.

Hot-glue a large protea (or other attractive bloom) and a piece of wasp's nest to cover the gap between the larkspur stems. Hot-glue the silk pods and the moss-covered twigs under the ribbon area, then fill in the area with the roses and globe amaranth blooms. Arrange a few clumps of moss and another wasp's nest piece around the remaining surface area of the wreath and hot-glue them in place.

Fragrant Simmer

When the fish you fried last weekend is still making its presence known, or when you just want to freshen up your home, spend a few minutes making this simmer for wonderful results.

■

Materials

Lemon peel, whole cloves

■

Instructions
Designer Tips

Fill the bottom of a 1-quart microwavable container with the peel of two lemons and 3 tablespoons of cloves. Add 2 cups of hot water and microwave on high until the liquid comes to a boil. Microwave for two more minutes on 50% power, then remove the container and place it in a location that will benefit from the fragrant steam.

Popcorn Frame

Children's art deserves to be framed in something as original and festive as their work, and this popcorn frame fits the bill. As long as you have a low-melt glue gun, this project is a perfect way for children to pass a bad-weather day.

Materials

1 bag microwave popcorn, matt picture frame, marbles, glue gun

Instructions Designer Tips

Microwave the popcorn as directed by the manufacturer. Hot-glue a single layer of popcorn to the picture frame, taking exceptional care not to burn yourself when working with small pieces. Arrange the marbles around the frame and hot-glue them in place, then fill in any gaps with additional popcorn.

The graceful curves and vibrant colors decorating this crystal vase contribute to its natural beauty. Microwaved grapefruit, lime, or lemon slices would look equally as nice.

Materials

Vase, wheat stalk, orange slices, dried floral blooms, green fern, small leaves, pods, short length of grapevine and raffia, glue gun.

Instructions
Designer Tips

Tie the grapevine around the vase with the raffia. Next, cut the wheat stalk down into several short lengths and tie them to the neck of the vase with another piece of raffia. Dry the orange slices in the microwave as directed on page 14. Last, arrange and hot-glue the oranges, flower blooms, leaves, and pods in place.

Embellished Vase

Vine Fancy

Most craft stores now carry a fanciful selection of shaped vines — from wreaths to arches to triangles — that can be decorated in minutes with a glue gun and a collection of colorful dried flowers and herbs. The oregano, apple slices, and zinnias all dry well in the microwave.

■

Materials

Vine form, zinnia blooms, oregano blooms, apple slices, globe amaranth blooms, stems of foliage, wire ribbon

■

Instructions Designer Tips

Working on the bottom edge of the vine form, hot-glue a base of dried foliage stems, using the illustration as a placement guide. Next hot-glue sprigs of oregano blooms on top of the leaves. Now add the zinnias, apple slices, and globe amaranth blooms, positioning them at unusual angles in the foliage. Tie the ribbon into a bow and hot-glue it in place.

Herb Butters

These versatile butters can be made with fresh-cut herbs from your summer garden or from a bundle of herbs from the grocery store. They store well in the freezer, so you can use them year 'round. The butters are especially nice to share with family an friends — take them in a small jar to the hostess as a gift or squeeze the butter from a pastry bag into beautiful patterns and shapes for your own entertaining.

Materials

4 sticks of butter,

1/3 to 1/2 cup of fresh-cut herbs

Instructions

Designer Tips

Chop two sticks of butter into 12 or 14 squares and place them in a microwavable container. Microwave on 50% power until the butter is softened. Repeat with the remaining two sticks.

Soak the herbs in water to remove any dirt and cut off the stems. Place the softened butter and the herbs in a food processor and whirl until the herbs are finely chopped and the butter looks light and fluffy.

Fill four containers (about the size of a baby food jar) with the butter and garnish with a sprig of fresh herbs. Or, fill a pastry bag with the butter and squeeze the shapes onto a sheet of wax paper. Refrigerate for at least two hours before serving to allow the flavors to set.

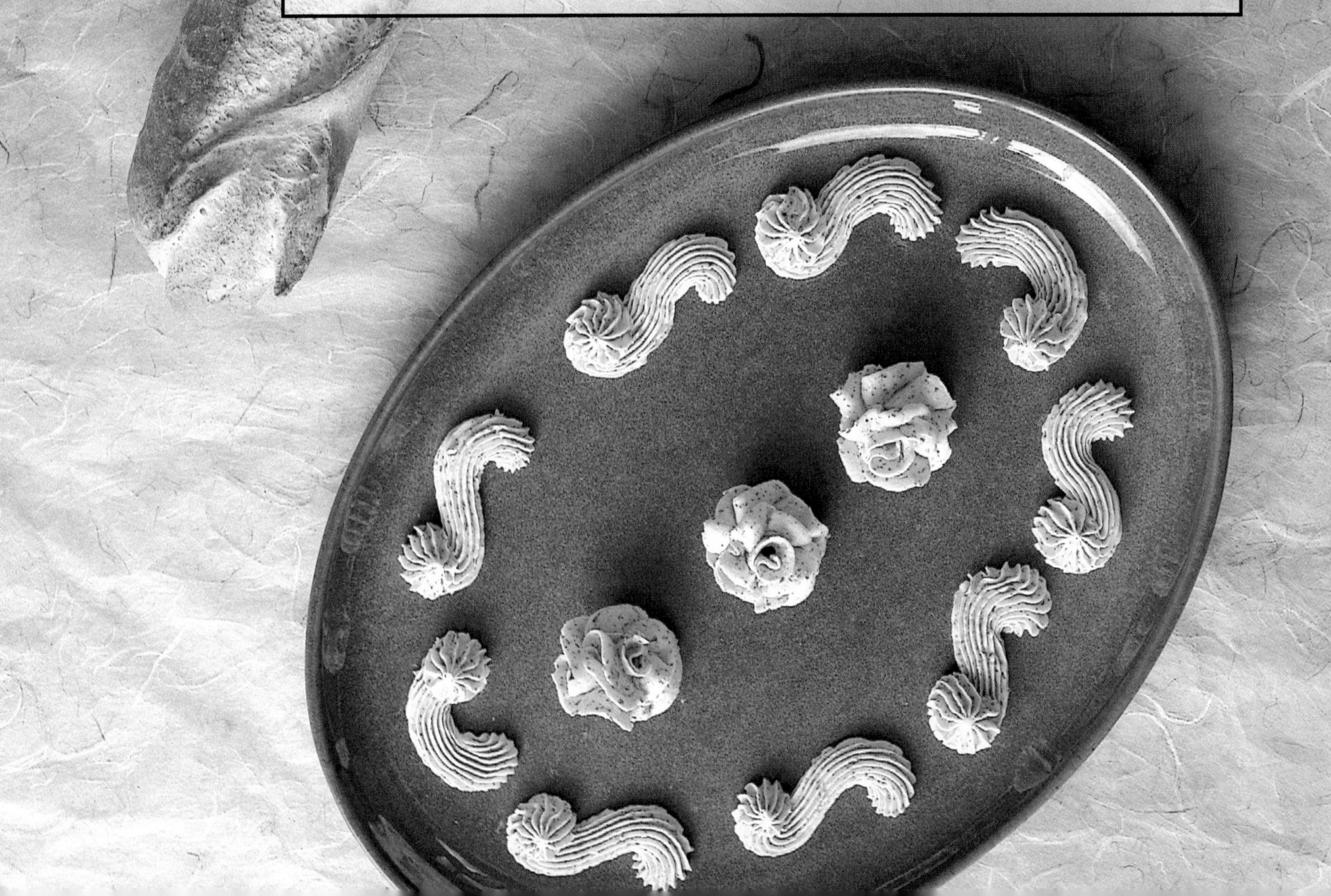

Cone Ornaments

A few minutes with a glue gun makes it simple to display some of nature's loveliest cones and pods as tree ornaments. If you don't have time for a leisurely nature walk before the holidays, check out the extensive cone and pod selections in craft and floral supply stores.

■

Materials

Cones and/or pods, gold ribbon or cord cut in 7-inch (18 cm) lengths, rosebuds, glue gun

■

Instructions
Designer Tips

Microwave the cones/pods and rosebuds as directed on pages 18 and 19. Fold the gold ribbon in half to form a hanging loop and hot-glue the two ends to the top of the cone, then hot-glue a single rosebud to cover the two ribbon ends.

Sundry Cone Wreath

Versatile cone wreaths can be made just from cones, or decorated with lavish print bows, which look especially nice during the harvest and winter holiday seasons. Dried flower heads can also be hot-glued around the wreath to add a sprinkling of bright color.

■

Materials

Cones in assorted shapes and sizes, 16-inch (41 cm) base, Spanish moss, floral pins, floral wire and/or glue gun

■

Instructions

Designer Tips

Arrange the largest cones around the wreath base. You can choose to arrange them very symmetrically or to vary their angles and placement. The cones can be attached with floral wire, hot glue, or a combination of the two. (See appendix for details of these methods.) Continue adding cones to the wreath until you've covered the entire surface, saving the smaller, more delicate cones for last. Tuck small pieces of Spanish moss into any spaces between cones to prevent the bare base from showing.

Popcorn Wreath

A fun crafter's motto for this wreath might well be, "glue a few, eat a few; glue a few, eat a few." The popcorn base works amazingly well with the glimmering gold ribbons and berries shown here, as well as with such winter holiday items as cranberries, tree ornaments, and red ribbon.

■

Materials

Straw wreath base, 2 bags microwavable popcorn, 2 lengths of ribbon in contrasting colors, 6 sprigs canella berries, moss, glue gun

■

Instructions
Designer Tips

Microwave the corn as directed on the package and set aside 20 or 30 of the largest pieces. Hot-glue the popcorn to the top and side surfaces of the base, then fill in any bare areas with the reserved pieces.

Hot-glue the berries to the top of the wreath base in a circle shape. Tie one of the ribbon lengths into a bow and hot-glue it to cover the area where the berries' stems meet. Loop the bow's streamers down the sides of the wreath, hot-gluing as needed. Weave the second ribbon through the berries and the bow. Last, hot-glue a few small clumps of moss around the berry and bow arrangement.

Harvest Arrangement

When they've been preserved in the microwave and prepared with craft picks, ornamental gourds become wonderful decorating materials for wreaths and arrangements. The delicate greenery in the basket is preserved olive branches — the perfect symbolic touch for a Thanksgiving centerpiece.

■

Materials

Basket, floral foam, craft picks, moss, small ornamental gourds, stem of silk foliage, preserved olive branches (or another silvery foliage such as silver king artemisia), glue gun

Instructions

Designer Tips

Cut a square of floral foam to fit inside the basket and cover it with moss. Secure the foam in the basket with hot glue. Dry the gourds as directed on page 15, then glue the non-perforated end of a craft pick into one end of each gourd. Trim the silk foliage into several short stems and insert them into the foam. Next, arrange the gourds around the basket and secure their positions by inserting the perforated ends of the craft picks into the foam. Last, insert the delicate olive branch stems into the foam to fill out any bare areas.

What could be lovelier than a holiday tree shimmering with the natural beauty of citrus ornaments? The ornaments are simple to make, and you could easily make several dozen extra to give as holiday hostess gifts.

■

Materials

Grapefruit, orange, and/or lime slices, assorted natural materials (pepperberries, rosebuds, German statice, globe amaranth, caspia, and olive foliage were used here), assorted trims for hangers, glue gun

■

Instructions
Designer Tips

Dry the citrus slices in the microwave as directed on page 14. Fold a short length of gold cord or other hanger material in half and hot-glue it to the back of each citrus slice. Play with different arrangements of the dried materials, then hot-glue them in place.

Citrus Slice Ornaments

Gourd Heads

Remarkably, both the projects shown here — the doll's head and the finger puppet — were made from the same type of gourd.

■

Materials

Gourd, drill, acrylic paints, small paint brush, knife or small saw

■

Instructions
Designer Tips

Dry a gourd as directed on page 15. Decide which type of head you want to make and cut off the appropriate parts of the gourd. For the puppet, the elongated top of the gourd forms the nose area, while this same elongated area forms the neck for the doll's head. Cut a finger-sized circle in the side of the gourd for the puppet; or, for the doll's head, allow about 1/4 inch (6 mm) of neck area and cut off the remaining portion of the gourd. Sketch facial features onto the gourd with a pencil, then paint with acrylics.

Traditionally, cornshuck dolls were popular because the materials were easy to come by, and a special doll could be made with virtually no expense. Today, cornshuck dolls are enjoying an increase in popularity with newfound interest in traditional handcrafts.

Materials

30 - 40 clean, white cornshucks, cornsilks, dental floss, small foam ball, white glue, gold pipe cleaner, optional embellishments (a small vine wreath base, greenery, and dried flowers were used here)

Instructions / Designer Tips

Fold a large towel several times to form a work surface. Soak the cornshucks for a few minutes in warm water. Place the foam ball in the center of a wide cornshuck. Fold the shuck over and roll it tightly around the ball so no foam shows, then twist the shuck at the top and bottom. Bring one twisted end down to the other and bind them together tightly with floss. (Your work will look like a balloon with a long tail.)

Arrange two cornshucks next to each other with their narrow ends overlapping in the center and roll them into a cigar shape. Tie the ends of the cigar shape to form hands. Pull the "tail" section of head apart and insert the center of the arm piece up against the head, just at the neck. Bring the tails back down and use several folded pieces of cornshucks to criss-cross over the head and arm piece to form a padded upper body.

Create the doll's skirt by arranging cornshucks (narrow ends facing up) around the waist and securing them in the waist area with several wraps of dental floss. Trim the skirt's hemline until the doll stands balanced. Drip some glue over the doll's head, then dampen the cornsilks and work them onto the head, using the glue to fashion and style the cornsilk hair. Finish with a light spritz of hairspray. Cut two wing shapes from large cornshucks and fasten them to the back with glue and pins.

Wrap and tie a narrow band of cornshucks around the waist to cover the floss, and cut any cornshuck tips that protrude above the waistband. Next, bend and shape the arms, and then pin them in place to dry. Open the skirt and place the doll on a paper cup to dry. When dry, remove all ties and bindings, decorate with flowers, baskets, brooms, etc. Remove the pins from the wings and decorate the joints with dried flowers. Retrim the hemline husks for balance if needed, and finish with a light spritz of the entire doll with hairspray.

Cornshuck Angel Doll

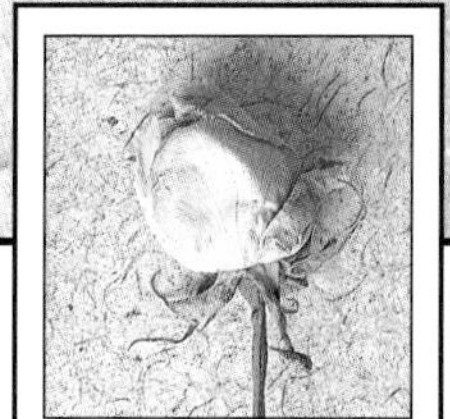

Cornshuck flowers make a beautiful, handcrafted alternative to run-of-the-mill silk flowers. If you're not happy with the finished shapes, simply dampen the shucks with water and reshape them.

Cornshuck Magnolia

Materials

8 cornshucks, cleaned and dampened, 30 - 40 3/4-inch-wide shuck strips, dampened, needle nose pliers, embroidery needle, dental floss, green floral tape, thin-gauge floral tape

Instructions / Designer Tips

Fold a large towel several times to form a work surface. Cut four spoon-shaped petals 2 inches (5 cm) wide and 5 inches (12 cm) long, then cut four more petals 2 inches wide and 4-1/2 inches (11 cm) long. Bend one end of a length of floral wire into a U-shape, using pliers if needed.

Arrange the strips together in a neat pile and mark their center. Press the strips into the U-shape, then pull both ends of the strips up. Catch the tip of the U with the pliers and pull the wire tightly down over the shuck bunch and spiral it down the wire length. Trim off any protruding wire. Tie off the bunch. Fringe the strips with a needle and then cut them down to 2 inches to form the flower's center.

Arrange the smaller flower petals evenly around the center section, tying each one in place as you go. Tie on new floss and arrange the larger petals, one at a time, over the gaps between the smaller petals, making sure to pull and tie tightly enough to compensate for the size shrinkage that will occur as the husks dry. Place one end of floral tape over the floss and make two turns to cover the floss. Spiral the tape down to the end of the stem. Push the petals back and down to expose the flower's fringed center. When completely dry, spritz with a light layer of hairspray.

Cornshuck Flowers

Cornshuck Floral Spray

■

Materials

11 cornshuck strips 1-1/2 (5 cm) wide, thin-gauge floral wire, white glue, pliers, dental floss

■

Instructions / Designer Tips

Fold a large towel several times to form a work surface. Cut the floral wire into ten 2-1/2- 3-inch (5 - 7 cm) lengths, and tear the cornshucks in half to form 6- x 1-1/2-inch sections. Fold the cornshucks in half lengthwise and tie them in a double knot. (The knot will become a flower bud.)

Place a dab of glue on each length of wire and pierce the double knot of each cornshuck with the wire. Tie each bud to the wire stem with a length of dental floss. Cut off the excess shuck at the end of the wire. Overwrap the floss tie with floral tape and continue wrapping to the end.

Attach the remaining bud to the tip of a 10-inch (25 cm) length of wire as you did the others. Overwrap the floss tie with floral tape and spiral down the stem for 1-1/2 inches. Add the remaining buds on alternate sides of the 10-inch length of wire about every 1-1/2 inches, catching each one with a few turns of the floral tape. Gently bend and shape the buds until you're happy with the look, and finish with a light spritz of hairspray.

A few minutes in the microwave oven after braiding and stitching saves days of drying time, and lets you enjoy your finished piece right away.

■

Materials

4-inch (10 cm) round wood base, drill, 100 long-leaf pine needles, strong thread, darning needle, shellac, small paint brush

■

Instructions / Designer Tips

Drill holes around the edge of the wood base about every 1/4 inch (3 mm). Soften the pine needles by placing them in a pan and covering them with boiling water. After 45 minutes, pour off the water and wrap the pine needles in an old bath towel. (If you can't finish the basket at one sitting, wrap the unused needles back in the towel so they will remain soft for several days.)

Tie six pine needles together with several strong knots just under the bottom edge of their caps. Divide the pine needles into three sections and make the first braid. Add two pine needles on the right side and make the next full braid. Continue braiding and adding pine needles until you have added 90 groups of pine needles, then continue braiding for approximately eight more full braids. Tie off the braid with thread and trim the pine needles close to the knot.

Thread the sewing needle with a 1-yard (.9 m) length of thread and attach the braid to the wood base using an overlapping stitch, taking care to hide the beginning knot. Continue stitching approximately every 1/4 inch, always pulling the thread tight between stitches. Continue stitching until you have four rows of braided needles, ending over the starting place so the rows will be equal.

To form the handle, fold both cap ends in toward the center and stitch them together. One end of the handle will already be attached to the basket; stitch the opposite end to the adjacent side of the basket.

Dry the basket in the microwave for 4 minutes on medium power. Place a paper towel under the basket, cook for another minute, and open the door to allow any steam to escape. Repeat the preceding process, then cook for another four minutes. Allow the basket to cool for 30 minutes, then immediately cover the inside and outside of the basket and the handle with shellac. Adjust the handle's shape if needed and allow the shellac to dry completely before handling.

Braided Basket

Appendix of Basic Craft Tool and Techniques

Many tools and techniques used by nature crafters originated with florists, whose needs for quick, reliable tools that are inconspicuous in finished projects have generated a market of versatile, inexpensive tools, tricks, and gadgets. These tools and techniques are well suited for a wide range of materials in addition to flowers — fruits, vegetables, nuts, vines, and cones — just to name a few.

Bases form a sturdy background and shape to which craft materials can be attached. Although the most common bases are in the form of circles, for wreaths, bases also come in arches, squares, rectangles, and many other shapes. Base materials vary, from foam to straw to vine, to name just a few.

Floral Wire

Floral wire comes in a variety of gauges, ranging from very thin and pliable (fine-gauge floral wire) to very thick (heavy-gauge floral wire). For larger projects, such as covering a wreath base with miniature bouquets, you may wish to purchase the wire on a spool (often referred to as spool wire). You can also use wire to create new stems for blooms that are too short and/or too weak to otherwise use. To do this, simply place a length of wire against the stem so there's as much overlap as possible. Then secure the two by wrapping with floral tape. Always wrap the tape down the stem at an angle and stretch it slightly as you work for better adhesion.

Floral Picks

These versatile wooden picks have a short length of fine-gauge wire attached and are used to secure stems of flowers or foliage that are too weak. The end of the pick is precut at an angle to make perforation into the base easier.

To attach stems to a floral pick, position the pick against the stems so the pick extends about 1 inch (2.5 cm) below the stems. Wrap the wire around the stems once or twice in the same place, then spiral the wire down the stems to secure the pick and stems together. Trim the stems where the wire ends. If the stems are especially fragile, add strength by wrapping the picked stems with floral tape. For materials like pinecone flowers that have no natural stem, you can create a stem from a length of floral wire, secure it to the item, and then use the floral pick as you would with a natural stem.

Craft Picks

Craft picks are floral picks without the wire, and they're used primarily to attach materials such as fresh fruits and vegetables to a craft base. The sharp end of the pick easily perforates the fruit or vegetable, and then the protruding end is hot-glued into a foam, straw, or vine base.

Floral Pins

These U-shaped pieces of curved wire look and work like old-fashioned hairpins. To use one, position the materials you're attaching against a straw or foam base, placing the pin's prongs over the materials and pressing it into the base at an angle.

Floral Tape

Floral tape comes in two varieties: a thick, strong tape (also known as adhesive floral tape) that resembles electrical tape, and a thinner, more elastic tape that's usually referred to simply as floral tape. The first variety is used to secure foam for arrangements in its container and can be substituted with any other strong tape, if desired. The second variety comes in several shades (such as brown and green) compatible with natural materials and is used to strengthen picked bouquets, or in conjunction with floral wire to lengthen and/or strengthen single floral stems. (For instructions on how to do this, see "Floral Wire" above.)

Glue Guns

Glue guns come in two varieties (hot melt and low melt) and in numerous sizes and shapes. Hot melt glue guns have been around for years. They're fast, versatile, and the only challenge in using them is avoiding the painful burns they can cause. They tend to be less expensive than the low melt varieties, but after a few painful burns you may decide the expense is minimal. Low melt glue guns are relatively new to the market, and their glue melts at a temperature so low it can't burn the skin, although it requires special glue sticks that tend to be more expensive than hot melt glue sticks.

No matter which variety you choose, you will continually be amazed at how quickly hot glue sets and at the endless number of items it will attach. Because the glue dries so fast, it's important to play with angles and positions before you pull the trigger.

Index